Young Wings

Gertrude S. Ward

Gertrude S. Ward

VANTAGE PRESS
New York

FIRST EDITION

Published by Vantage Press, Inc.
516 West 34th Street, New York, New York 10001

Manufactured in the United States of America
ISBN: 0-533-12245-7

Library of Congress Catalog Card No.: 96-91007

0 9 8 7 6 5 4 3 2 1

To all those who supported me and eagerly
and graciously lent their assistance in many ways

Contents

Young Wings

Memoirs

I thrust my pen into my soul,
    And there found diverse shades of color
That blended into perfect whole,
    A book containing all my memoirs.

As I read each line on line,
    A whisper soft as breath did say,
"Drink, this is the ripe sweet wine;
    Write, many souls will pass this way."

Inception

A light came forth on Mercury's wing,
    And lodged itself in a darkened womb;
Knew the mission its ray would bring,
    And struggled to pass from out its tomb.

To form it pressed with a strength its own,
    Endowed with potential to fulfill;
To hosts of heaven its destiny known,
    And heaven to witness the Father's will.

The Ballet of the Leaves

The stage was set with several baring trees,
  Some short, and some quite tall;
The ceiling draped with gray-blue canopies,
  Cov'ring October's fall.

The exit of the birds and other noise,
  Had quieted each pew,
The orchestra sat in a stilly poise,
  Waiting for the cue.

Readied for, "The Ballet of the Leaves,"
  In crispy rustling gowns,
Of yellows, red, (a bit of green to tease)
  And variegated browns.

The instruments of wind blew a blast,
  Up the curtain rose,
Hushed audience, and revealed the cast
  That Mother Nature chose.

To the accompaniment of the gusty winds
  Began the lively dance,
Conducted by the trees' own swaying limbs,
  "Pomp and Circumstance."

The Dance

They spread across the ground
    With grace and practiced ease,
And often twirled around
    When carried by the breeze.

They took two pompous strides,
    Then hurriedly retreated;
One made a circle wide,
    All this was then repeated.

The one who played the lead
    Joined with a romancer,
Then from his arms was freed
    To join another dancer.

Back to her lover's arms
    She came with hesitation,
Wooed by his great charm
    To reconciliation.

Enraptured with her prize,
    She fell in his embrace,
Then was lifted to the skies
    With lightness and such grace.

In three great sweeping whirls,
    Each one a little lower,
      She paused—
Then took another twirl,
    This time a little slower.

The Finale

Then suddenly and without warning,
    A leafy chorus glided in;
The biggest tree was now performing,
    To join the show for one last spin.

"The Ballet of the Leaves" did end,
    With a solemn bow and pause;
The closing scene became quite darkened,
    And the rain was their applause.

Plea for Love's Constancy

I wake, O God, to dream no more,
    Commune with me upon my bed,
For my wandering days are o'er,
    All lesser loves lie cold and dead.

Prove me now that I may know
    The sweetness of Thy tender caring,
Woo that I may feel the flow
    Of Thy love, ever sharing.

Call to me from pleasure's den,
    Wherein unknowing I have lain,
Speak to me in stillness when
    My eyes know tears, my heart knows pain.

Sing to me love's sweetest song,
    Engraved upon Thy love-filled heart,
Sing and love and woo as long
    As I shall need Thee for my heart.

Hail January

Hail January! Infant of the new-born year,
On your warm hearth new hope has brought a ray of
     cheer,
And with that flickering hope, you smothered all past
     fear.

The many struggles in pursuits you left behind,
You willed to understanding hands to be refined;
Disguised you mete out countless blessings to mankind.

Your blithe soul has charmed the ardent optimist,
With greater dreams his eager heart could not resist,
To aid his often feeble will to dare persist.

In the heart of winter scenes you plant your seed
Of hope, and beckon to the distant sun to feed
That hope, until the fruit fills full the object's need.

Hail January! Press your dreams into the year,
Press them hard while there is yet a ray of cheer,
Press them oft with hope to gladden all the year.

Symphony in Embryo

Sing soul, unleash your prisoned Vedic hymn,
in splendorous, raptured rhythms yet unsung:
reach out to touch the spreading wings of dolphin,
and from thence, with greater speed be flung
to bright renown'd Cygnus,
canopy of all our stars, and eye of northern heaven.
Command that it be blessed emissary,
for a virtuously holy leaven,
'til all heaven resound and then return,
to thrust my soul into a larger song.

Coo On

Mourning dove rest 'til the night be full spent,
Deaf yet is the town to your mournful lament.

Your hidden life that is under my eave,
Has filled me with wonder, pray tell me your grieve.

If brooding o'er nestlings has been your deep moan,
Be thankful their wings had strength to be flown.

If injured by love then speak your complaint,
Unburden yourself from the weight of restraint.

If west winds have blown too fierce at your door,
Then nestle thee down, just a little bit more.

If your lay be a treatise on heaven's creation,
I beg you coo on, dove, your hymn of oblation.

A Bird's-Eye View

I soar me up to catch the view,
 Of a bright and jaded world,
And in the ocean of my blue,
 A beauteous world becomes unfurled.

The trees in all their various cast
 Wave leafy arms to each newcomer,
Stalagmites in the winter's blast,
 Umbrellas in the summer.

Shaded valleys are fine frescoes,
 Embedded like inverted domes.
Mountains? New worlds, I would suppose,
 Where bears and chipmunks hide their homes.

Flowers in their dazzling colors
 Lie like jewels in rich green velvet,
And the sparkling water's contours,
 Lie stiller than an amulet.

As beauty of this world I view,
 With practiced eye on either side,
I'll sing my song with impromptu,
 In chirps and tweets of lusty pride.

The Angel's Hand

One morning I woke up surprised
    In a frosty fairyland;
The joyful scene before my eyes
    Was painted by an angel's hand.

The pines were heavily dusted
    With a powdered sugar coating;
The children's wagon I feared rusted
    In a frothy sea, seemed floating.

The roofs were iced like layer cakes
    Ready for a birthday party,
And heaping higher with snowflakes
    Was the broken fence at Marty's.

Huge gumdrops topped the sawed-off stumps,
    Looking good enough to eat;
Hollowed footsteps outside the door,
    Were footprints of our daddy's feet.

The dog next door had left his tracks,
    Evidence he was trespassing;
The bushes all had whipped-cream backs,
    Lower branches were caressing.

Enraptured with the pictures yonder,
    Made by the angel's artful hand,
I lost myself in childish wonder,
    In a creamy candyland.

The Child Philosopher

Crumpled quilt upon the sheet,
cribside down;
booties lying in the drawer,
dirty clown:
images not yet set,
nor sequented with faltering steps.

The child mind, in one grain of time
leaps from warm dependence to philosopher;
Innocent of sage's ploddings
laboring to find the child they lost.

Night's Inheritance

When sun has left a crimson trail,
When dusty purple hues prevail,
    They leave their rich inheritance
    To weary earth's gray bushed expanse.

The magic power of the ray,
That fed the blossoms for the day,
    Was folded in the flower's sepal,
    To keep the hungry bee's cup full.

It willed again, but not for long,
The cricket's monotonous song,
    And teased the aimless firefly,
    To demonstrate his single eye.

It made the brooks a bit more bold
To chant their allegories fold
    On fold, to the darkness creeping 'round,
    Giving creatures room for sound.

It pushed the stars out all *en masse,*
And with their patterned shiny glass,
    Gave the mariners a certain chart,
    To guide the ships with their star-art.

It left the distant needle spire,
Again reluctant to retire,
    Pleading in a restive mood
    For greater light, and lasting good.

Cool twilight hours, invested with
Fine substance for the writer's myth,
    Have cradled half a world to sleep,
    Hiding busy days in that great deep.

Prayer of Intercession

Oh, holy passion, I weep, I weep;
    When will this cup of myrrh be drained,
That in my secret lace I keep,
    So willing for a world so stained?

Can this weeping much avail,
    Empowered by my loud invoking?
Surely such prayer must prevail,
    That fills my sleep and crowns my waking.

To the Children

Oh, children dear, your cheerful way,
With love has blessed me many a day;
    I kiss your brow and stroke your hair,
    With heart uplift I say a prayer;
      I bless your helpful little hands,
      And pray to fill your soul's demands.

How oft I held you 'til I felt,
That with my heart, yours too did melt
    Until there was a knowing union,
    Touching each in sweet communion;
      Not always by the spoken tone,
      Yet all the same 'twas plainly known.

Ofttimes quiet I see you muse,
Upon a subject that you choose;
    Your unexpected welcomed praises,
    Have touched upon so many phases,
      And firm rebukes have made me see,
      How much more careful I must be.

I try to know your busy mind,
The thoughts you think, and what their kind;
    I find them varied in your dreaming,
    And sometimes I see them scheming,
      But I never cease to give God thanks,
      Even though I know you're full of pranks.

With tossed up hair and eyes that shone,
You've told me just how much you've grown;
    All day long you play at will,
    Your anxious step seems never still;
      You dash about with such commotion,
      When e'er your mind is filled with motion.

From morning's dawn 'till setting sun
Our lives are blended into one,
    And as I kiss your pillowed head,
    And stoop to bless you on your bed,
      I tell you of the Christ within,
      And hope that you will think on Him.

Little Boys

Sticky hands and dirty face,
    Peekin' 'round the cellar door,
Leavin' footprints o'er the place,
    On the clean waxed kitchen floor;
      Those are little boys.

Toys all strewn about the house,
    Rings around the bathroom sink,
Sometimes scurrying like a mouse,
    Or sitting quiet when they think;
      Those are little boys.

Holl'rin' when you wash their ears,
    Wigglin' when you comb their hair,
Cryin' when they're full of fears,
    Or poutin' in a corner chair;
      Those are little boys.

Lovin' when they feel the mood,
    Shoutin' when they're good and mad,
Eatin' when they like their food,
    Jumpin' when they're mighty glad;
      Those are little boys.

Little Girls

Screamin' when you comb their curls,
    Fuss to get their ribbon straight,
Dressin' up like grown-up girls,
    Impatient when they have to wait;
      Those are little girls.

Mimicin' their mother's ways,
    In a fashion kind of sweet,
Playin' house for endless days,
    Pretendin' baby is asleep;
      Those are little girls.

Generous when they feel the mood,
    Sobbin' when their feelin's hurt,
Worse than any funeral dirge,
    And sometimes play a little flirt;
      Those are little girls.

Subtle on their father's knee,
    Haughty when they want their way,
Helpful when they care to be,
    And angels when they pray;
      Those are little girls.

Nature's Touch

Beneath the rustle of the willow leaves,
    Half-hung in ribbons o'er the shadowy stream;
I sat in stillness waiting for the breeze,
    To whisper confirmation of my dreams.

Pale daisies, untamed monarchs of the lea,
    Bowed in obedience to the gentle breeze;
And from my grassy throne plain did I see
    The timid lark swoop down to play and tease.

Frail buttercups like drippings from the sun,
    Made cheerful accents in the daisy bed;
Where they laid their golden heads upon
    The brown earth, to gaze upon their fountainhead.

The jay that sought my statue company,
    Chirped accents in that language universal;
While to lapping waters danced succinctly;
    In this stately palace concert hall.

Intrigued I watched it soar, with skillful grace,
    So free it flew the ether waves, that bird;
Whose instinct sought fulfillment in its chase.
    'Twas then a haunting song of love I heard.

A song that harmonized with nature's whim,
    Rehearsed in whispers through all things God made;
A song that distances could not bedim,
    To echo in the hollows of the glade.

It hinted of both pain and joyous pleasure,
    Pleasure soon released to deeper pain;
That swallowed up in one uncertain measure,
    A fading faith, then raised its song again.

This time a little surer, a little stronger,
    It lifted song and wing into the air,
Singing clearer and the measure longer,
    With no hint of struggle or despair.

I graced the purple clover at my side,
    With touch as light as silver wings of bee;
'Twas then heaven's portal opened wide,
    And angel whisperings trickled down to me.

Aspirations

If my song seems to you simple,
  And my music somewhat bland,
If my mood has shades of purple
  As my thoughts pass through my hand,
Know that in my sundry dreaming,
  I had wished them to be grand.

All of worth that I did glean
  As I passed from year to year,
I discretely sought to preen
  Each line to fit the falling tear;
Not that tears of myrrh might shine,
  But that the pearl of price appear.

When clever verse my mind conceived,
  Heart would often countermand,
Because it had in part achieved,
  A knowing of the thing at hand,
And with this greater attribute,
  In greater excellence it planned.

When each sequence had its course
  Of the after and before,
The ink could not spill forth the words
  With so frail a pen, nor
Could the weighted heart, though filled
  With a forceful word and metaphor.

And when each passing episode
    Was painted on the pure white sheet,
The tints into each other flowed,
    As the chaff bends with the wheat;
Instead of songs of nightingales,
    There seemed a faint uncertain bleat.

When all the tears were dried and set
    Into meters, rhymes, and parts,
And all the gleanings played upon
    The taut lute strings of other hearts,
I prayed the wine sipped yesterday,
    Might pour a blessing on their hearts.

Companions

Come sit with me beside the weedy pond
    Where the ducks have gathered for a conference,
And tell me stories of the magic wand,
    'Til sparrows leave their perch upon the fence.

Run with me down the pastures rolling green,
    And hear the crush of grass beneath our feet;
Yesterday 'twas where the cows had been,
    Just beyond, was where the sheep did bleat.

Please wander with me through the caves of rock,
    To test the volume of our echo,
And count again the treasures in our stock,
    But be careful of the pit below.

Race with me to the barn and climb the hay,
    In our jeans we'll slide the whole way down,
It was put there fresh the other day;
    We'll have lots of time before sundown.

Help me bait my line some noon for fishing,
    Or roam the woods for flowers we think rare;
Perhaps we'll learn just what the birds are wishing.
    And feed on ripened berries that we share.

Call for me as you pass this way to school,
    I'll carry all your books along with mine;
Together we will all our lessons pool,
    Compare our notes before we reach the pine.

Stroll with me, Jennie, to the old stone well,
  Drop a penny in and make a wish,
But let's promise that we will not tell,
  Because to you, I might seem very foolish.

Meet me down beside the apple orchard,
  Just beyond the fence and hollow tree;
To speak the rest it seems a little hard,
  And right beneath the window I'm not free.

May I hold your hand, dear, in my own,
  As I ask you to the farmer's dance?
I had never noticed how you'd grown,
  'Til the other day I stole a glance.

I've known you long but now my tongue is tied,
  All I can do is stutter as I say,
I ask you, Jennie, will you be my bride,
  When roses lend their sweetness to our day.

The Clock in the Hall

When Dad for the night has coddled his Chevvy,
    And the sounds of the children have ceased
At a moment when eyelids grow heavy,
    And the house has been folded in peace.
        The clock in the hall,
        Stood a brave sentinel.

With the last heavy tread of feet on the stairs,
    The clock in the hall heard the chimes
On the porch playing musical chairs,
    And faithfully beat out the time.
        The clock in the hall,
        He slept not at all.

The mouse from the chilling cellar emerged,
    To dance a wild "Tarentella,"
'Til a gong in the silence surged
    And scared that imp of a fella.
        'Twas the clock in the hall,
        That ended his gall.

The spider that conjured his fanciful art,
    That the maid was sure to despise,
Kept weaving his part upon part,
    Heaping evidence for his demise.
        Said the clock in the hall,
        "By the broom he shall fall!"

Just moments before the dark midnight hour,
     Twelve bells could be heard through the wall;
The gongs in the old village tower,
     Had bellowed a mocking reprisal.
          Yet the clock in the hall
          Was moved not at all.

The damsel who took to being out late
     Gave the timepiece a moment's suspense,
When she paused at the door with her date,
     Then whispered some soft words in French.
          The clock in the hall,
          Understood not at all.

One night beneath the west window was heard
     A cry that put shadows to flight,
The me . . . ows were so dreadfully slurred
     That the moon retreated from sight.
          Still the clock in the hall,
          Made his hourly call.

Things that he heard, and things that he saw,
     Were sometimes beyond what we dream of.
His performance ne'er had a flaw.
     What more could be said of
          The clock in the hall,
          That brave sentinel?

Tribute to a Rose

Fair rose, your secrets I would beg of thee,
Unlock my bosom for your company;
    No other bloom has given such delight,
    Nor sung as many love songs in the night.

I love your perfumed sweets and condiments,
Distilled in hues, and robed in elegance,
    Alone, a queen serene you often pose,
    With none to equal you, oh, lovely rose.

As fair matron of the summer bower,
You are the firstling of the bride's new dower;
    So versatile, no special day you spurn,
    Nor shun the spreading arms of woodland fern,

Your precocious thorns cannot debar
Your timely bloom, nor leave an unkind scar
    Upon your velvet plush, caressed by sun
    And kissed by dews before the daylight come.

The artist's canvas garnished with his brush,
Has painted dreams in ardent eyes that hush
    The lips of fools and rush the poet's blood,
    To laud the virtues of your bloom and bud.

Then why not I your tender beauty claim,
And add another praise to their refrain;
    I would seek to be the God that made thee,
    Fair flower, if my heart were bent to envy.

Love Concealed

Great muse, where hidden now your savored tongue
That fails with heart to make a paragon?

Rend now love's rapture from its fleshly cell,
And with its strength all hosts of heaven impel

To wing it to the object of its care,
Let drop love's disposition everywhere.

Fain would my tongue come forth from its concealment,
And make this pen a willing instrument.

'Tis is now chained solely to my own heart's knowing,
(Lest, to love's object, perchance it may be showing).

Yet deeper feels this heart than tongue can frame,
So for this cowering tongue I feel no blame.

If tongue has lost the art of such revealing,
Then heart alone must bear the deeper feeling.

Press then more fluent bard to pen its lay,
Or some sculptor form it with his clay.

Ode to the Arbutus

Arbutus, when I heard your name,
I wondered why you had not fame;
You cannot hide your buds for shame,
    So delicate are they.

I love the scent of your pale pink,
Small, smaller than a baby's wink,
Innocent, yet so distinct,
    Cradled where you lay.

Around deep moss and stone you creep;
'Neath tall green blankets, there you sleep,
Hidden by the grasses deep
    Like a stowaway.

Your kingdom in the spring expands,
As you embrace the earth with bands,
Holding in your viney hands,
    That tiny pink inlay.

Your paths are chosen from the start,
By captains who their journeys chart,
That wind up anchored in my heart;
    You have a *charming* way.

The Intangible Wind

Courageous wind, breath of the almighty,
You have built an unseen sanctuary
Where I meditate your diverse ways;
Your peace, your fierceness, and your sudden calm.
    How may I measure your capacity,
    Or reproduce your formless pageantry,
    Your sudden visitations, bold delays,
    That lift the sturdy oak, yet sway the palm?

You sweep across the ages of earth's time,
Dance in the hoary caves of yesterday,
Incense cold brine to curl, lash out, declare
Its haughty vehemence to the harmless shore.
    Between bare rocks proclaim your shameless whine,
    Leave glaring havoc of your reckless way,
    You slam a chamber door behind a prayer,
    Creep stealthily along a rustic floor.

You tease the innocent with your caprice,
Evade with mocking glee the outstretched hand,
Goad willing feet to run with you, then flee,
Leave no charted path for them to follow.
    Eternal breath, where do your wanderings cease,
    In artful halls of space or burning sand?
    Marshall now your secrets, tell them to me,
    As you told them to the migrant swallow.

Illusions

Draped in flesh men come alone,
and struggle in their prison walls of blood and bone,
until the inner strife becomes a quickening prayer,
the prayer that goads them into worlds unseen
by mortal eyes, that only know earth,
and its manifold illusions.
Life supreme submerged in flesh
(that grows in greater density within the form)
knows itself the life that never had been mortal born;
nor can the chains of death do more than set men free
to know, the life does live eternally.

The Awakening

I dreamed a dream, but in my waking,
 The very same descending light,
On my consciousness was breaking,
 As had filled my perfect night.

I held this new descending calm,
 Compassed with such whisperings sweet,
That breathed upon me like a psalm,
 And made me feel at last complete.

'Twas not the selfish flesh that bound
 With a passion to possess;
Too much with spirit interwound,
 And all senses acquiesced.

Suspended in a hallowed sphere,
 With angels standing in the space,
Their ministrations being sincere,
 Left no will to mar the place.

If heaven was the instrument
 That compounded such a rapture
To make such perfect complement,
 Then heaven also must it capture.

The prince that stirred the sleeping beauty
 On the pillow where she slept,
Did also touch her earth completely,
 'Til every atom in her wept

Out the sleep, and implanted
	In each cell, a lens for clearer seeing;
The effect being absolute,
	Sealed the intertwining.

Death and Rebirth

Death's shadows ride upon tempestuous seas,
but wisdom sees her fruitless stirrings shake
illusory walls, that crumble at their moorings,
to wash away a will that sought its own
unholy way. What then, when this relentless
saline yield shall give its seeming all?
Summon hope (the infant food of faith)
to fill the hollowed breast and raise
a fountainhead of life, to build anew
with faith, a structure of reality,
that other men will feel and know as truth.

The Glen and the Guide

The beautiful spot at Watkins Glen, New York, at the southern end of Lake Seneca, is one of the favorite places of the author. The railroad bridge perched so high above the glen is no longer there.

I

You, now standing at this gaping portal,
In wonder gaze, and breathe a bit immortal,
   Awed by the megalithic structure,
    Adamant and towering o'er;
   Read there time's chiseled grandeur,
    A hieroglyph of ancient lore.

II

Look up before you, travelers, and see
The bridge arched graceful in its masonry,
   And fashioning it on either side,
    Apothecary jars, assorted,
   Outdoes the mason's pride
    And by no plan of his supported.

III

Some fifty, sixty feet of them or more,
And from their tops the green herbs spilling o'er,
   No pharmacist so well supplied,

(Such beauty heals) it is no wonder
That the soul is sanctified,
    As you look and pause to ponder.

IV

Those sentinels upon the bridge will change,
To watch the view they shift and rearrange;
    Each does unawares perform
      A mystic watch upon the wall,
    Weaponless, diversiform,
      Innocent of protocol.

V

Now we too are sentinels as they,
Plainly you can see the gorge array,
    The waterfall, the churning tide,
      So buoyant here, will for'er be still
    Upon that film. On either side,
      Name each formation as you will.

VI

Down there the giant's foot, to stop the flow?
Foolish one to think he could do so,
    Deter he can, but never hold
      This relentless torrent's beat,
    And just ahead the cascade bold
      And confident performs its feat,

VII

Leaps from that pinnacle and threadlike falls.
It startles some, and others it enthralls.
    A spectacle, that needle's eye
        From whence it drops just o'er the path
    To the cavity below,
        To make a showy aftermath.

VIII

These tunneled stairs lead to the upper gorge,
Where deep canyons only time could forge;
    The stream from here is barely seen,
        Almost sepulchered and shut,
    Often have I wondered too,
        How the stone so smooth was cut.

IX

As we walk along this quiet vista,
Notice the marked difference in the strata,
    Its thinness and excessive chipping,
        Shaped roughly by the elements,
    And the water's constant dripping
        Adorns the sides, between the rents.

X

That leaning ash above with stride from cliff
To cliff seems not to fear a fall, or if

The leafy causeway be undone;
  Some day it may complete the task.
O'er there ne'er shines the sun,
  The shadow here, too deep is cast.

XI

"Hush," a Keats in contemplation there,
Midst a labyrinth of path and stair
  (With balconies and cliffs o'erhung
    With trailing greenery). This stream,
  Where soundless clouds have flung
    Their imagery, he weaves his dream

XII

With golden words. What to the touch seems hard,
Is softened in the spirit of the bard.
  What beauty was the world denied
    By that young poet pressed for time?
  May this one by his pen applied,
    Give sweetly that lost cup of wine.

XIII

Notice now the sun is fuller play
Shining on cathedral walls, steel gray;
  Hallowed out by what great act
    Of providence? What weakness here,
  Yielding to some strong impact,
    Making this so large a sphere?

XIV

What did divest it of its furnishings,
And leave undone the broad pool's burnishings?
 The broken altar so impounded,
  Lying in the resilient flow,
 Is better here so grounded
  Than in the narrow gorge below.

XV

The verity of ages here expounded
In the strata, emphasized, compounded.
 Can you hear the booming console
  Thundering out the great Amen?
 The azure dome receives the whole,
  Then the silence fills again.

XVI

Ah, the pools, of all this lovely glen
I like these best, must be some eight or ten
 Of them, each with a magic potion:
  One to wake a latent gift,
 One to capture lost devotion,
  One to mend a lover's rift,

XVII

One for inspiration, one for joy,
One to charge the feet of some small boy.

Scallops circumscribe this one.
  What matter if they be of shale,
With the scallop overdone,
  And the lace a little pale?

XVIII

This group lying like cups is for effect,
Each one on a shelf, so like a set.
  'Twould seem that nature meant to be
    Deliberate, and to drive the point,
  Each trickled by a small degree,
    The lower chalice to anoint,

XIX

Falling with a minimum of stir.
That one, the needle's eye in miniature.
  And ever guarding this young motion,
    Looms the brother of the sphinx
  In a faithful mute devotion,
    Undisturbed when sparrows drink.

XX

Here the glen, more rambling and less steep,
And foliage from each jutting ledge does creep.
  On this moss a bee half sits,
  Making it a parlor chair;
  Unused to comfort, moves in fits,
    And on that stone an elfin pair:

XXI

A lovely place for them to romp and roam,
With a thousand nooks to make a home,
    With elfin steps for elfin size,
      And a brighter light to bless
All their labors, I surmise,
      And to secure their happiness.

XXII

Before us now is Jacob's ladder rising.
(That little sigh is not surprising.)
    The climb is hidden from your view,
      Pan's indulgence covers all,
With intent to overdo,
      Whether or not 'tis ethical.

XXIII

Here, frayed ramblings spreading well beyond
The proscribed borders, like some vagabond.
    That railroad bridge so very high,
      Emerges like a pencil mark
Across the opening of the sky,
      Poised like a doting patriarch.

XXIV

The busy-ness beyond this diverse green,
Interject their sounds on this serene.

From here you may your steps retrace,
  Or climb the ladder as you will,
One leads to your starting place,
  The other to atop the hill.

Peace

Peace has a virtue all its own,
    And by that virtue wields its power
To crush the head of fear unknown,
    In moments of the *would be* hour.

O'ershadowed peace will favor all
    In need, in mute, yet active will,
But peace possessed will not so fall,
    It waits a moment to distill

The drops in fertile soil, prepared
    By searchers who pursue its calm;
Where balanced law has been declared,
    There it wields its balm.

Compelling peace will mock the course,
    Of opposite polarities,
And impregnate with silent force,
    To bear the likely child of peace.

Peace touches all related parts
    With a velvet hand unseen,
Gently folding in its aura
    All who walk where it has been.

Genesis

Deep, deep, dark stillness,
Soundless, motionless,
Impotent stillness,
Endless, formless deep,
And somewhere there was God!

Deep, deep, breathless void,
Incognizant void,
Helpless, senseless void,
Boundless, barren womb,
And somewhere there was God!

A breath swept through that void,
The waiting womb vibrated,
And then received His Spirit;
The womb, no longer barren,
And God was omnipresent!

God omnipresent!
Gone the endless void,
Gone the barren womb,
Gone impotent deep,
And all was God!

"Let there be," he spoke,
Light swallowed darkness,
Sun, moon, and stars awoke;
Formless breath became
A universe of Light!

The Uses of Nature

I

What man is there, but by the sun enticed
did plant his seed, renew his vow,
and emerge from out his self-made hermitage
to feel Sol's kiss fall on complaining lips,
converting them to anthems?
The ray, that by divine intent to illuminate,
has also purpose to unleash his lips
and mellow all his world.
Is there ought could bless him more or better
in infirmity or cheerless days?
Has not this golden light
served to effect a greater faith,
where faith had begged to wane—
even to the minor note of the defunctive rite?
Would such a man a worship curse
that proclaimed the sun his deity,
call it heresy, and scorn its God?
Let us ascertain the solar benefits and thinking say:
"This has made me more an uncomplaining man."

II

Dark night descends, to hold earth in majestic stillness,
revealing countless patterns in the sky.
What man is there would mock its influence?
Would not the night's serenity,
impugn his blasphemy,

and make it seem the more adverse?
Oh, let him listen for the muffled tread
of angels' feet in passing o'er,
and poise a contrite heart
on concepts lofty as the blessed stars.
The fevered brow that feasts on energies
has felt their touch, cherished it
as ointment from the galaxy of stars,
and proved a medicine of charm.

The night will testify of ancient myths
rich in allegories, bold in truth,
folded in each constellation.
Each seeks an artistry upon the heart.
With breath as deep as night, let him speak out,
And to a listening universe assert,
"This has made me more a peaceful man."

III

See the sepal parting to release
the essence of the flower to the bee,
waiting for the sweetness,
or leave its scent upon a lonely myrrh,
to provide a holy washing for the sorrow;
as the rainbow's spectrum
oft repeated in the diamond dew,
gives promise of a cleansing to the leaf.
Contemplate the pulsing of a stone,
interacting with the light
to glory in its character;
declare it too a living thing.
Strong too, the rock, shaped to fit a setting

holding up all things to the face of heaven,
so that mortals may come face to face with God.

Watch the eagle lift his potent wing
ever upward, reaching for the sun;
could not God impute a counterpart within His image?
Has He made man less than the creature?
And see the blithesome humming bird
that has borrowed wings from Mercury
to compensate for size, to secure his own defense,
then weaves with delicate endeavor,
that masterpiece among the summer leaves.

You have seen the seagull dip his hungry bill
into the convex surface of the crest
to snatch his repast from the restless sea.
Who would deny those birds were not endowed,
and say their talent balanced not their need?

Ponder the perception of the tendril
to find its way to raise a morning glory vine,
reaching to the mark most opportune,
selfless guiding the recumbent vine.
It looks not down upon its greater weight
to dissipate its energies in sighs,
but from the sun a courage takes
to match its blossoms with the sky.
Who will look wisely to these benefactors and declare,
"This has made me more a thinking man."

IV

How many lovers have there been
to sit beside a prating brook,
that boasted of the many kisses there reflected;
then washed the secret with the image,
to keep clear the magic flow?

In the waterfalls there is the sense
that somehow earth is weeping,
and you wonder at the tears that fall
into pools of peace too deep for show,
or manifest in churning discontent;
both patterning humanity,
yet giving of their best to calm
a weary mind and soul.
How many are the ones who seek a respite
searching out a haven through the tangible?
Would not a man so touched
give praise for such a flow,
and by it make him more a grateful man?

The Lonely Poet

The vision broke upon him in the early morn,
A flash of wonder all his being did adorn,
And only he did know a poet had been born.

He had a sweet communion all that night,
That fed his contemplation through the light,
But who else heard the words that filled him with
    delight?

He felt the pulse of meters in his quickened blood,
Words came rushing through him in a driving flood,
But who else knew that God had opened up a bud?

Rhymes and meters found expression day by day,
Into unpretentious verses pressed their way,
Alone he sought the science of the poet's way.

The tender love he felt for all became unfurled,
In line on line that with adjectives were pearled,
Like a knowing overlaying all his world.

Revelations that he gleaned upon his bed,
Were to him a feast of nocturnal bread,
And silently—
He hoped that some would understand what he had
    said.

The Dimpled Child

A mother listened quiet
  At the patio door,
Where her dear Annette
  Played upon the floor
With her playmate, Violette.

The mother at her mending,
  The children at their games,
Aristocrat pretending,
  Even changing names,
Busy borrowing and lending.

The mother never spoke,
  The children chatted on,
Shaded by the oak;
  One in Mom's chiffon,
The other in her mother's cloak.

The mother changed her thread,
  The children changed their hats,
Violette sweetly said
  Like a diplomat,
In a voice less spirited;

"I never mentioned it,
  How did your dimples grow?"
Annette answered definite,
  "My mother prayed them so."
The mother sewed, and smiled a bit.

Twin Flames

Proem

His soul was rising through his eyes,
    And she read with tender care;
      In spite of quiet depth,
Nothing there to analyze,
    Thoughts and longings standing bare;
      She could touch the feeling,
    That reached out into the air.

All his thoughts seemed open highways
    On which they traversed with great ease,
      Pressing firm upon her soul,
Without the tongue's delays
    To find the proper words to please;
      They left a silence deep,
    Like a nun upon her knees.

I

They met, not within a garden wall,
    Or some poetic circling of magnolia
Trees, watching o'er a festival
    Nor in ivied halls of academia,
Where the youth build up their dreams and prate,
    In the atmosphere of ephemera.

II

It was a moment neither could foresee,
　　But those who watched beyond the silvery stars,
Knew the hour of that expediency.
　　So is the nature of all avatars.
To see the need then precipitate,
　　In the waiting soul's vernacular.

III

Such descending on her being was new,
　　That hidden sphere was drawing from somewhere
An essence, like dry earth absorbs the dew,
　　And both minds gave the same thoughts to the air;
As nature in her workings reciprocate,
　　With their perfect counterparts and share.

IV

Appearances of manners, face and eyes,
　　Matched not with these inner absolutes.
The outer sees a face once known, then pries
　　It from a hiding place, or mind playing mute,
Gives up the search to abrogate
　　The thought, because it could not execute.

V

With such sureties, each time they met,
　　The thing she could not see, became

The once familiar, drawing like a magnet,
　　And inly she called out a given name,
The present one could not substantiate.
　　That inner made so definite a claim.

VI

That unseen voice shouted, "Verily
　　We knew each other in a time gone by,"
Simple and without complexity.
　　She listened for a word to verify,
The name slipped easily in to captivate,
　　But the mind refused to clarify.

VII

It anchored deep within the airy spaces,
　　Between the present and the long ago,
While angels peeping through their trysting places
　　Whispered, but remained incognito,
Waiting anxiously to mediate,
　　In spite of busyness from to and fro.

VIII

Pure contentment cancelled out the need
　　To struggle with the temporal fickle sense;
Like some battle with a dying creed,
　　To keep the thing intact by strong defense,
That which only served to separate.
　　This counterpoint with peace was too intense.

IX

Twenty thoughts trying to find a mold,
    Brought twenty questions pressing hard behind;
In his reverie did they unfold,
    Where she lost sight by the interwind?
At some point the two must consummate
    Into the pattern destiny designed.

X

Mind echoed on through ages of the past,
    Through the columns of the Parthenon,
And in some dusty abbey overcast
    By ruins, too remote to think upon;
Or did he in some forest gladiate,
    And fall victim to a sword he died on?

XI

To her he was a Galahad of old,
    That thought fit well into her blest content;
His character was of one high-souled,
    And that knightly poise was evident.
Such a knight would seek to elevate,
    And this he did with, "You are radiant."

XII

Was there a time in a pastoral setting,
    Uprooted for a stoney work of art,

That spoiled the beauty of the summer setting,
  Where they had loved each other with full heart?
No place seemed to elucidate,
  Past and present being too far apart.

XIII

Time can be cruel or benevolent,
  But for her it worked a miracle,
For each encounter laid a precedent,
  To set the next upon a pinnacle;
While her soul stamped out the duplicate,
  And made her willing heart a chronicle.

XIV

Had he read those deep ethereal lines,
  Of heart and soul refusing a forgetting,
That eyes could not make clearer by all their shines,
  Nor by the fullness of any lip's begetting?
Then it came, almost deliberate,
  Each pearled incident a separate setting.

XV

Twice he said, "I never will forget you,"
  And her heart drank up that first blest phrase,
Then—did she his inner meaning misconstrue?
  But—he sealed it with a paraphrase.
Was this something he did meditate,
  Or a professional's impromptu?

XVI

There were many things she knew about him,
 And could speak them as though they were her own;
None were clouded by the interim,
 And such eloquence of undertone,
Nor by sounds around less delicate,
 But protecting like a wall of stone.

XVII

She thought she saw angels smiling sweet,
 Watching from their high blue citadel,
While still clinging to their mercy seat,
 Listening for some mortal's urgent call.
Clever how they could anticipate,
 Two purposes so diametrical.

XVIII

No dream it was when waking from a sleep,
 She felt him stroking gently her low brow,
From his eyes the feeling dropped down deep,
 His lips spoke softly, "How are you feeling now?"
Nothing better could facilitate,
 A path between their beings, or allow

XIX

His gentle thoughts to glide adown unhampered
 In the transport, by any listening ear

That might misjudge intent of a spoken word,
    When even angels stood by to revere;
The emanations were immaculate,
    And all thoughts etched forever deep and clear.

XX

The kiss he longed to give her brow was found
    Instead, rounded in his azure eye,
Then fell on her soul without a sound,
    Where angels left a mark to sanctify,
And forever after to reverberate,
    In the caverns of ethereal sound.

The Unveiling

1

O'er his tedious work the apprentice was stooped,
    With his hand to his work and his eye most intent
On the prints that his master had so neatly grouped,
    And the wise man who watched his firm hand so
        unspent,
Became pensive in mood and his dim eyes did droop.

2

As the youth slowly reached for his thin camel's hair,
    That he poised with great care o'er his unfinished
        task,
His master leaned back in his worn swivel chair,
    That supported it well by the dusty wine cask,
While the early rays played on his ledgers that glared.

3

His thoughts burrowed deep but not verbal was he,
    As he sat in the silence that was kin to his muse;
He lost all conception of time by degree,
    At such times his habit it was to peruse;
Now the visions before him, humanity's sea.

4

In procession they came, good men, merit bedecked,
   With pride of their years and experience too;
Their cold metals, all tarnished by time that had
      checked
      Their glitter and could not suffice for the new,
Were pinned to their vests with ribbons select.

5

Then on came the misers whose breastplates were gold,
   But beneath them beat faintly their cold hollowed
      hearts;
That were drained of compassion and love; now behold,
   How they stoop as they fittingly play their proud
      parts,
Not guessing how much they had lost in such selfish
   mold.

6

The elite in the crowd followed close on their heels,
   All bedecked and bejeweled for society's page;
Their proteus dramatics were by far most unreal
   And more ostentatious than plays on a stage.
What tragedies there would their bared hearts reveal?

7

The mad loves of the wordy made show of their ware,
    Contesting all issues with high-sounding phrase,
With discords unfit for the bosom of care;
    Their breath turned all cold from such mental craze,
Deficient in thought and unholy in prayer.

8

'Twas here the old man tapped a tune on his chair,
    And his lips barely moved as he formed the word
      "masks,"
Then repeated his words with a hint of despair;
    Yet only he knew that their sham could not last;
The humble would learn and the wise would take care.

9

Dispersed in great numbers marched partners in stride,
    Some fearful, some hungry, some sorrowing in tears,
Some weary, some fallen, some stripped of their pride.
    Some prayerful, some youthful, some bent with their
      years,
Of all that passed by these had least they could hide.

10

The clock on the cluttered-up shelf had struck nine,
    And the sun on the ledgers had moved its broad ray
To the sleeve of the youth for a moment's recline.

The cold shadows of masks fallen dead in the way
Were the symbols of faces that hid the divine.

11

The employer arose in the mood of his muse,
    And slowly he paced to the side of the youth,
"My son," he began—
"As a steward of time I suggest that you choose
    To know yourself well and to seek after truth;
And knowledge with wisdom, pray never confuse."

12

Now philosopher's eye with apprentice's did meet.
    "Many the man who has hid from himself,
And only perception can see his retreat."
    Now the young man ne'er knew what the old man
        did mean,
But the light in their eyes matched their hearts'
        quickened beat.

Sonnets

On Faith

Great faith, eternal, primal element
Ever active has its abode in man,
And with it all the decades he may span;
Without the use of it does much prevent.
The elements he names portray intent
To build or nullify as human can,
Or melt 'til all be made more puritan;
Of faith effects are born and frugally spent.
How great our faith to build? The quality
Of consequences? Incipience to fall?
Could men embrace this grand reality,
He then would comprehend himself, annul
All ill effects 'til gloriously free,
To march with faith, the element eternal.

On Destiny

In all our living there rings an holy chime
Of destiny, but only bellowings
Reach our ears—through our meanderings—
That fade the sweetest echoes of the chime.
Destiny hides itself in folds of time,
Ov'rspread with the gauze of temporal things;
By listening not for God's great answerings,
We pass heedless over things sublime.
Verities we bury with the prize,
Forfeiting the glory of the feast,

And raise instead the things that we surmise,
As though the verities had been deceased.
We stumble on the stone of compromise,
While standing full before our own high priest.

A Hidden Pearl

All our lives we search for one grand line,
To weave through decades like a silver thread;
A bit of wisdom like an arrowhead,
Embedded in a context to enshrine
So it will not lose the hyaline,
Nor the thought to which it was so wed.
Posterity may deem it merited,
And posterity preserve the shine.
Yet if through oft repeated use it should fade,
Or break off like a thread with too much wear,
Other men may pluck it from the shade,
And in a novel phrase again declare
The selfsame jewel, but this time unassayed,
To leave to future years to prove the wear.

The Virtues of Music

It's true that music soothes the savage breast,
    And we've seen a babe's eye slowly close,
    Leaving play behind that sleepy pose,
While slipping from this world, to one more blest.
One sees emotions rising to a crest
    Blotted out with pianissimos,
    When soft sounds and rhythms interpose,
Until one finds oneself, more self-possessed.

Music soothes a broken heart or will send
    A love dart deeper, without knowing where
To strike the last tone to the destined end.
    It prompts a meditation or a prayer,
Or could be all of these in just one blend
    But following the laws of laissez-faire.

The Song of the Sirens

The song of the sirens has caught my ear,
E'en the wild waves are stilled to hear;
   The caves repeat, bewitchingly sweet,
The Sirens' song as my bark draws near.

What song is here sung that my passions compels
To lure from the world, the sea, and its perils?
   This uncertain beat, in my heart does repeat,
I hear, but hear not the saga it tells.

I feel, but know not what lurks on this shore,
What joy or what sorrow composes the lore.
On this rocky main, what joy or what pain,
To soar as on wings, or rise nevermore?

More wont to the sea and its perils I've been
Than conscious of heaven's sweet grace. So then—
My crew, to the mast, tie these feet fast,
And sail like a charger broke loose from his pen.

If to the mast, my mind with my feet,
In cowardly fashion is making retreat,
From the deep I must learn, 'til heaven I discern,
Charge then the wild waves, 'til all fear I defeat.

The Poet's Worth

Who shall sing the poet's song
    When the poet is no more,
And would not the land be dreary
    With no song from shore to shore?

But you ask, "What worth the poet?
    His profession seems so frail,
And we have our friends for parties,
    We also have the nightingale."

Oh, my friend, how gay your party?
    I feel you do the poet wrong.
What would be the use for singing
    Without the words to fit the song?

Our sweet nightingale sings only
    In the night for his own wooing;
The poet is daylight picks up
    The strain where he left off his doing.

Shy lovers would not do so well
    If there were no words to sing;
They need sweet words to lean upon
    To assist them in the faltering.

We shall sing the poet's song
    For this time and evermore,
So the land be not so dreary
    With no song from shore to shore.

Time Is Not

Father Time has once again
    Folded carefully his cloak;
On his face he wears a strain,
    For now he hears the final stroke;
      The midnight hour that steals its way
      Into infant moments of new day,
      Calmly echoes, *time is not.*

Hidden in his inner vesture
    Where perception's eye can see,
Is carved an image of the future,
    Ofttimes formed quite carelessly;
      Unmindful as he made his cast,
      That his creation knew no past,
      But lived on, for *time is not.*

The dreams he cherished now and then,
    He thought had faded in the new,
And builds again he knows not where,
    But silently selects the view;
      Careful now to not parade,
      Lest once again the picture fade,
      Still unmindful, *time is not.*

The prophecies he reasoned out
    Have failed again to prove him right,
His ego suffered in the bout,
    His words became a dreaded blight;
      A feeble effort to retrieve
      Discarded words that he believed
      Echoed on, for *time is not.*

A bit more wise, yet not quite sure,
    He bids the infant year to yield
A crop that will effect a cure;
    He spreads his vision o'er the field,
        Looks to the future with a hope,
        And hints he sees a broader scope.
        Years have taught him, *time is not.*

A Trilogy

The Pessimist

Who is this man who sleeps in yesterday,
whose eyes refuse to open with the sun?
Beneath imagined clouds he walks, his mind
acclimated to his sculptured shadows
that he displays with gusty pride to men
more bent to cheer or youth. Ever feeding
on his discontent in generous proportions,
reveling in premeditated mutterings.
His ears more trained to lions' roars, do fail
to know that lions have no song to cheer.
When sun has pulled its dusky curtain down
To close the day, he never sees the stars.

The Optimist

This man hangs his sun in cloudy skies.
Impartially it shines and spreads its ray
on all his fellow men, and then returns,
transformed, to bread he thankfully receives.
Those who watch the feast ne'er comprehend
that his sumptuous table was created
by his sanguine expectations, conveyed
by natural law, that finds its heritage,
then manifests itself to meet his need.
He cradles roses with a tenderness.
Though withered in his arms, praises them,
And gently lays them down to view the stars.

The Knower

The wise man sees his road was ever paved
with benign assistance day to day;
the gains and confidence of yesteryear
that fed his ego self were plainly seen
as the shell of his accomplished merits,
and all adversities now proved his good.
In this knowing was conceived the knower.
Now comprehending with the light of heaven,
he fashioned every moment with great care;
no longer pressed his optimistic doctrine,
nor wallowed with his pessimistic friend,
But sustained his life in one eternal dawn.

Nameless

One omniscient will poised itself
in the calm of infinite expanse,
(the Alpha and Omega of all things)
quivered joyously with His power to create,
His wisdom to be just,
and His love eternal, to sustain.
Eager to extend His selfless self,
the voice of the eternal breathed out to infinity,
"Let there be Light."
Light that would forever be perception,
The Eternal eye.

One breathful ray sped on
to fill that boundless void.
The Light now omnipresent!
Need we ask, "Where art thou?"
"All of heaven cannot contain Thee. . . . "
Where is there place where Thou art not?

One primal pulse trembling into form
rocked a cradle orbit into being;
spread royal robes with velvet elegance;
linked each to each in vibratory oneness
until all was softly touched.
The hands of the Creator.

All now was made eternal motion,
and in rapt delight reverberated
like a symphony of many spheres
to be played upon the stars,
before the throne of the eternal,

and in the ears of cause.

Oh, breath of the Almighty,
You have and will forever live.
no longer do I think of you
as Life, or Light, or Love alone,
i recognize you as a pulse I cannot name,
a touch, intangible but real,
That tells me surely that you are!

Smile, Sweet Babe

Sweet babe, smile your little smile,
As I hold you this short while,
    Long since my babes have left their nest,
    And with them, all that was the best.
Smile, help fill that space that since was left.

Those large eyes that hold so steady
On my face, have turned already
    All my heart and will toward you;
    They speak so plainly from their blue,
Like the infinite is pressing on me.

What better grace could God bestow
Than let me sit in that blue glow,
    And now your smooth and tiny hand,
    Refuses mine as contraband,
Heaven's portion being enough for you.

So, you waiver your good-bye,
That's quite alright, I read your eye;
    I will not press you to earth's will,
    Because it's plain that you are still
Living half in earth, and half in sky.

The Soul of You

I felt the balm of healing love,
That rested on me from above;
    You brushed my brow as you stood by,
    And as I looked into your eye
      I kissed the soul of you.

Then in response I felt your heart,
Had sent to mine a subtle dart,
    Releasing there a love so pure,
    And one that had become mature
      Within the soul of you.

In your eyes that wore a smile,
That rested on me for awhile,
    And made me sense a calm repose,
    As does the dewdrop on the rose,
      I felt the soul of you.

Your gentle touch and quiet way
That rested on me many a day,
    I found in all I saw and did,
    I found them in the words you hid
      Within the soul of you.

I felt those words in sky and sea,
And heard them chant in harmony,
    Two souls joining now as one;
    Then when all my day was done,
      I held them in my soul.

The Chalice

I perceived the thought of God toward all,
the thought was love continually.
As love issued forth it embraced all forms,
and each form He tried in His own fire;
the fire that consumes all dross,
but augmented,
as each inferior thing is transmuted
by the violet flame,
that shines from out the spectrum.

I perceived the thought of God toward me,
and questioned my adversities.
many I called my trials,
my disciplines, my chastisements;
only vanity could make such claim.
I became cognizant that
God tested His own forms by degrees,
by His own strength,
His own love,
and His own endurance,
because there was no greater.

I perceived with a clearer vision,
we are His chalice,
we are His crucible
in which He tests Himself;
for in Him all sufferings must come to pass,
and all vanities be vanquished.
Now I understood more plainly Solomon's wisdom,

"All is vanity."*
and how the human is as grass that withers,
unless our God be manifest within,
For what is flesh, for that too must wither,
the trials I called my own,
those sorrows I endured,
have brought me one step nearer,
and for His sake, I hope to be one atom purer.

*1 Ecclesiastes 12:8

A Memory

There it was, pressed in the pages of a book,
a bit of periwinkle,
treasured from a day's short trip;
found behind an old stone wall,
where it ground its viney way
through a sparsity of earth and abundant shade,
where the southern suns crept through
to assist the shade and moisture,
to leave a deeper shine upon the leaf.
Now leaf and flower folded down,
where no sun can e'er peep through.

The blossom now is faded to a paler blue,
the green leaves denuded of the shine
and that perfect star no longer visible
but the memory still holds clear
of the place and time.

The spot was one of nature's own,
a part of Appalachia,
where the stone and river wound
and two structures turreted,
stood behind a wall expressionless,
overlooking all.
Though the flower faded,
and the chlorophyll less deep,
and the star passed out of sight,
the whole is still alive,
in the friendship of one dearer
than any earthly sight.
She is the one who said,

"This is periwinkle,"
and dug some from the very spot
for a corner of my garden.
Now when I ope' the book upon the page,
I draw deeply from her act of love.

Bouquet of Memories

Memories, each one a tiny world,
  With innocent beginnings in yesterday,
Tucked in the pages of a cherished book,
  As though to hold the mem'ry still that way.

A bookmark with a clover sketch upon it,
  And a bee sucking from the flower,
Could not taste the sweeter benefit,
  From the poet's garden, "The Lost Bower."

Even though beauty laid on beauty,
  And the vine and woodland traced so clear,
Offering creatures such amenity.
  Several pages past there showed a tear

So faint, it could easily be missed.
  Tears have that way, to fade and hide a pain,
Like the memory of one barely kissed,
  That could not forget, nor yet sustain.

A rose-pink ribbon from the senior prom,
  That brought such a flurry of excitement,
Now lay on a love poem prone and calm,
  To help it keep that youthful sentiment.

The periwinkle pressed so thin and dried,
  Left a sweetness in this house of treasure;
It lay leaf and blossom, side by side,
  While heart and mind played out each happy
    measure.

A four-leaf clover plucked from summer grasses,
Where we sat and talked of pleasant things,
Made a link in friendship, but alas—
For strength, the frail leaf to a sonnet clings.

Like photo pictures on the walls of time,
That lose their threads in a busy day;
These have left their touches in a rhyme,
To complete a memory's bouquet.

Complement

The song that vibrates in this breast
And leaps to lips to be expressed,
　　Echoes words of your blithe tune;
Your love sung in a major key,
Is counterpointed perfectly,
　　Like nature's melodies with June.

Is there a light within these eyes
That shines quite useless to disguise?
　　'Tis the reflection of your own;
And as I draw from you this shine,
So akin to the divine,
　　E'en by the angels it is known.

Covered with your spirit's balm,
I move like one within a calm,
　　While all my being shouts acclaim,
So potent to bring heaven down;
My peace serene, your jeweled crown,
　　Encircling like a silken frame.

Joy bursts these bands about my limbs,
And gives them will to touch the rims
　　Of galaxies, beyond the sun.
Your love my carriage of transport,
Leads to a queenly garden court,
　　Where walls with gossamer are spun.

My gown, the aura of your caring,
Reflects the virtues you are wearing,
    Tinted delicate o'er all.
Your love flows from these blessed hands,
Has muted all the world's commands,
    And transformed duty into call.

The Climb

I

The hill that rises from my window pane,
Wears a veil today of cloud and rain;
Sad it looks with such a heavy chain
    Of Gray, above the valley floor.

II

Just last eve the sun had slowly pressed
Its shiny orb into that rigid crest,
Without proving which was mightiest,
    Or claim the title Conqueror.

III

Mind retreated to more youthful days,
When enticed by summer's cheery rays,
I climbed upward through a woodland maze,
    Like one with duty to a chore.

IV

Only laughingly I climbed that mound,
Panting gladly for the sights around,
When quickly everything turned so profound,
    Above the woodland corridor

V

The churning stream made docile by the height,
Quieted all earth in the midst of light.
All moved softly with the cloudy white,
    Completing this grand mirador.

VI

I felt myself moved from the ordinary,
Expecting soon to hear an "Ave Mary,"
With atmosphere so ablutionary.
    Standing close to heaven's door.

VII

Descending into sound from all that stillness,
Time overlaying on the timeless,
You felt again the weight of busyness,
    And the mundane taking o'er.

VIII

The moments, all too brief when comparing
Earth's segmented hours, always tearing
Day into light and dark, never sharing
    As a whole, the day before.

IX

Other climbs had not so much of pleasure,
Too few the rests, and long the minor measure,
For the saddened song oft missed the treasure
    Hidden in the lengthened score.

X

When zealous clouds outwitted sun,
Hope crept through on an orison,
And fighting like Achilles' myrmidon,
    Climbed ever up the rugged tor,

XI

While remaining in a Stygian gloom,
Struggling for a light to disentomb,
My boundless soul from such a prison room,
    And to a resurrection soar.

XII

But when this victor triumphed and the prize
Shone less in hand than in my dampened eyes,
That mirrored also all the sweat and cries,
    I shouted, "Victory evermore!"

What Is the Matter with Charlie?

What is the matter with Charlie today?
He rests on my words whatever I say,
He teased not his sister the whole morning long.
She looks on that kindness as something so wrong.
    What is the matter with Charlie today?

He stumbled four times in just this one morn,
And fussed somewhat where his pants were worn,
You hoped his glasses needed no changing,
Or a messy closet he was rearranging.
    What is the matter with Charlie today?

He spent more time in the bathroom than usual;
Over *that*, his sisters had plenty to say;
"Mom, you ought to portion his bathroom time,
His session's enough for a whole lifetime.
    There's something wrong with Charlie today."

He ate *half* his food, so you thought him *half* sick,
Then the telephone rang, and he turned awful quick;
This made you think he was being deceptive,
With such a change from the contemplative.
    What is the matter with Charlie today?

He pretends to study, but I don't see the page
Turning at all in his small hermitage;
If he's at last so intent on his study,
Then why does his cheek keep turning so ruddy?
    Does Charlie have a fever today?

When I mention a girl is turning his mind,
He protests with a shrug and acts so purblind;
Now I have something with which to parlay,
Because I know what's the matter with Charlie;
The teenage dreamer fell in love yesterday.

A Home

A home is filled with many things,
Up to the attic and out the wings;
    A favorite painting on the wall,
    An antique clock still standing tall,
An old shoe buttoner and pieces of strings.

A game that packed the time with fun,
When evening hours pressed on the sun;
    A tool of some kind that no one knew
    What it was and what it could do;
And a faded pie ribbon that Mom had won.

A baby doll that lost an arm,
An iron pot from off the farm;
    A popular book with yellowed page
    That swept the country with such a rage,
And a warm quilt that kept its charm.

Lingering around an open fire,
Or looking out on the old church spire
    Piercing the orange of setting sun,
    Like a robed monk in saffron.
Waiting for the sultry day to retire.

But my favorite things are those
That can't be touched like the smell of a rose,
Like a home that is filled with hope and laughter,
And the tingle that lingers the morning after,
With the memory of someone who comes and goes.

Annunciation

Twenty white and twinkling lights,
    Festooning folds of evergreen,
Mixing with the yuletide sights,
    And a magic winter scene,

With twenty lights before my eyes,
    I hear again the heralding
Of Gabriel, poised in the nightly skies
    With his, "Fear not . . . " unto Mary.

Twenty lights cannot shine brighter
    Than that star o'er Bethlehem.
Nor can these points gleam whiter,
    Than stars in Gabriel's diadem,

Raying down to earth that night
    The message of the great Messiah,
Leaving hope in place of fright,
    And an angel's gloria.

O star of heaven, O hope of earth,
    We await the promises,
That once again will lift the darkness,
    That now so heavily enfolds us.

Affinity

Am I a twin to the wild ocean,
    With all the stirrings that it causes;
Then roars back to its own motion,
    Between the lashes and grand pauses?

When lashes of life sorely press
    Upon my heart with such emotion,
I may faint or wallow in excess,
    Rise or fall in the commotion.

Am I a kin to every flower,
    When I feel a warm affinity,
Gazing on some summer bower,
    Exchanging simple praise for beauty?

For when I touch their silky coat,
    I feel the touch deep down my spirit,
Joining something once remote,
    Like human to the infinite.

When the lark with song unique,
    Is strutting through the sunlit meadow,
Or singing lyrics through his beak,
    In an oft-repeated rondo;

I catch the lilt of his glad song,
    And try to mimic every note,
Then with a whistle pass along,
    The music of his golden throat.

Moonlight on the Lake

Moonlight on the lake,
a shimmering chalice,
fragmented by the ripple of the waters
stretches back upon a slate of blackness,
in a pyramid of light.
Each bar reaches to the shore
with a soft ripple on the stiff unconscious land,
to lose another and another bar of light,
absorbed by the greedy earth,
sucking it into the eerie stillness of the night.
Each ripple had a silvery shining moment,
and each performed exquisitely.

A Child's Eternity

All time dies in the heart of a child,
    When his bright eyes open to the glare of day;
By every glance he is teased and beguiled,
    And every object is turned to play.

There is no such thing as overtime,
    His play is lavished to the edge of sun,
Because all hours are one prime time,
    Like a full summer has just begun.

He has no concern for need or care,
    He knows only a broad eternity;
All thoughts and play are turned elsewhere.
    As he moves through his day-long odyssey.

At last from exhaustion or maybe duress,
    He is lured from his play to his nursery,
Is laid on his pillow all fetterless,
    Then slips to the other side of eternity.

Violets

Violets on the shaded lawn
    Hidden from the morning sun,
Have waited since the break of dawn,
    To flaunt their thousand blooms as one,
Not e'en a blade of grass slips through,
That violet carpet drenched in dew.

Hardly can the petals miss
    The gentle touches each to each,
And green swards for emphasis,
    Only shortens more their reach;
Befitting more some grand duke's garden,
Than any common citizen's.

Violets, what a broad array!
    And for fear of stepping on you,
We skirt the rim of your display,
    So as not to mar your virtue;
For we wish not to tread heavy,
On your Maytime purple beauty;

For a tenderness o'ertakes us
    Mixt with a mystic rendezvous,
And leap of gratitude strikes down us,
    To a world beyond our view,
A place of peace all crystaline,
Filled with attitudes benign.

Elementals glad but shy,
　　Dancing with a springtime grace,
Seem more at one than even I,
　　To be a part of your fair race;
But our sighs are one, and holy,
And we two, breathe charity.

In your copious purple presence,
　　The weave freely through your blooms,
Not in bold irreverence,
　　With liberties that one presumes,
But blessing like a benefit,
And a family closely knit.

Unrestricted, they sing silent,
　　Or else we miss the higher sound
Of their whispered jocund accent,
　　Because the human is so bound,
Hearing not the elementals' measure,
And guessing less than half their pleasure.

But when mowing day comes round
　　We will not spoil our own sweet musing,
By needless cutting of your mound,
　　And by it our own blessing losing.
And poets too, will form their line,
To add touches so divine.

When at last your time shall come,
　　Willingly you drop your cloak,
Until nature's pendulum,
　　Swings once more to May's first stroke,
Heralding your violet bower,
Prodded by each April shower.

Then once again we will resume
    The rituals we're accustomed to,
And elementals will assume,
    Their eager service to attend you,
And once again a poet sings,
Of violets and of holy things.

Affronted

Huge waves dashing heartily,
haughtily,
heedless 'gainst the giant boulders
with their diamond spray,
determined to unseat them from their ancient mooring,
and elutriate their soulless faces.
Splash and stare,
stare and splash,
one active and one passive,
one noisily affronting,
one adamant and mute,
unyielding,
determined to secure his ancient place;
each waiting for the wind to initiate a pause,
to rest their spirits.

My Echo

I have a faceless echo
    That sometimes follows me,
It has a little tremolo,
    That trails off where I can't see.

It mimics every word
    Like it has no mind,
But repeats what it has heard
    And sometimes not so well defined.

If I call a friend,
    To show her a new treasure,
It overtakes to apprehend,
    My simple utterance and pleasure.

Though it's fun to tease him
    From his hiding place,
All my prospects look quite grim,
    To ever see that ghostly face.

He bounces off the rocks,
    With much agility,
Behaving like a shuttlecock,
    And with the same effrontery.

He takes my private words,
    And makes them very public;
At least, if he has overheard,
    He need not play so lunatic.

His lack of social grace,
    Is something quite appalling
No one could make a legal case,
    With this fellow so enthralling.

In spite of all he does,
    I love that little fellow,
For he reflects all I once was,
    But now his echo seems more mellow.

And I am now more careful
    Of the words I speak,
And my attitude more prayerful,
    Lest he mimic my critique.

A Listening Angel

I heard a mother weep last night,
  Her teardrops shone as tiny crystals;
They held so much of love and light,
  It pressed into the intervals,

Where she spoke softly each dear name,
  And where 'twas heard, "I love you so."
She went on the same, the same,
  Between the tears and spirit flow.

There was no sound to break the mood,
  Only a hush to fill the night,
Where angels like a solitude,
  For the ministry of light.

The First Train Ride

Into the suitcase went all she could pack,
    Then pondered a moment her new liberty,
'Twould be some time before she'd be back
    To home and friends and her own big city;
"But I'll take some notes as I ride along,"
Or so she said, while her will was strong.
    She boarded the train,
    In a driving rain,
Midst flashes of light and a loud thunder crack,
Just as predicted in the "Almanac."

The first time alone her heart skipped a beat,
    This turn in her feelings she did not expect.
She felt her heart strike the back of her seat,
    'Til the conductor's click pulled her erect.
Her ticket was pinched in her taut little hand,
Clasped like a wing in an iron band;
    While the wheels spun 'round,
    With so steady a sound.
The farther she traveled from "Hackensack,"
The louder she heard the clickity-clack.

The conductor gave her a wry little smile,
    And spoke a few words to ease her care,
Then whistled a bit as he went up the aisle,
    And just about then the day turned fair.
The rain stopped beating on the window pane
And the sun peeked out on her former disdain,
    Like a magic cure,
    On discomfiture,
But the wheels still sang their clickity-clack,
Like an endless song on an endless track.

The beady rain on the window had dried,
    And the meadows now had turned bright green;
Like some fairy queen with her brush applied
    Had given the land a glorious sheen.
She had trouble keeping her eyes steadfast,
Because all objects were moving so fast;
    So the deep ravine,
    Was barely seen,
But was scary enough when you took a look back,
Yet the train sped on with its clickity-clack.

Quite far ahead she could see the wide bend,
    Shaped to the hillside's rounded curve,
Marking the land by the train's front end,
    And the power that gave it all its verve.
It curled around like a huge iron snake,
Slithering between the reeds and the lake;
    The smoke puffed out,
    Curling about
On the pristine blue in grays and bold black,
Trying to keep up with the clickity-clack.

So steady and firm the wheels made their round,
    She imagined them saying a thing or two;
There was nothing to distract the sound with sound
    But at that moment the train whistle blew.
Picnickers raised their arms to cheer,
The fast-moving travelers and engineer;
    The gates went down,
    On the edge of town,
The train pressed on with a bit of a slack,
Still pounding out that clickity-clack.

They rode through a tunnel a quarter mile long,
    And when they emerged the landscape was denser,
That was a sign she'd be there ere long,
        Then someone confirmed the town was called,
        "Spencer."
The captain appeared and startled them all,
When he looked down the aisle and shouted the call,
        "The next stop is 'Reading.' "
        That's where she was heading,
She heard the screech of the brake on the track,
And the slowing down of the clickity-clack.

There were people milling about the station,
    Some laden with luggage, some waving their arms;
She spotted her grandma with a smile on her face,
    That was always a part of her charms.
The clickity-clack then faded away,
And she imagined the joy that would end her day,
    But in dreams that night,
    Through the bold starlight,
She heard the wheels going clickity-clack,
While she sat on her grandpa's horse bareback.

The New Face of Things

It's all new, the lane displaced
And broader now, where we once raced
    Our 'cycles 'long the river front;
Now stone levees where the maples graced
      The river's flow. Our festooned wheels
      Hummed to the graceful mallards' squeals,
    By night to the frogs' obnoxious grunt
    That to the rushes made appeals.

The old schoolhouse stood staunch as ever,
But now was filled with new endeavor;
    Committee meetings of every sort,
And a colorful craft store for the clever,
      Each classroom made into a stall,
      Filled with do-dads wall to wall,
    (Charm or chaos, who can tell,)
    Now they call it the, "Mini Mall."

The corner drug store forever shut,
To make room for a Pizza Hut;
    So goes the rumor I've been told.
Gone the soda fountain but
      It was a bit dilapidated,
      And the facade antiquated.
    I'm sure that change is for the better
    With brick and mortar more updated.

On the edge of town the old feed mill
No longer stood below the hill;
    Instead, a complex high and grand
Trimmed 'round with bush and daffodil;

Pretty to the sight I must admit,
   But in my mind I cannot fit
That homey past in this grand setting,
   With the view so opposite.

I thought it might be fun to see,
The changes that had come to be,
   But pleasure mixed with disappointment,
Followed curiosity.
      Yet now I've found a new content,
      And never more will I lament
   The past I cannot bring again,
      For present blessings evident.

Imagination

(In memory of a neighborhood lad who came to sing to
    me in my backyard while I was recuperating from a
    broken ankle.)

He sat beside me, it was sweet,
This little lad just at my feet,
In his hand was a guitar—
The fret end near the jugular—
All made of cardboard and of glue;
And here and there a streak of blue.

He adjusted all the strings,
With a poise that reverence brings.
The frets across the fingerboard,
Were few and not so neatly scored;
Made of toothpicks (quite a trick)
And more glue to make them stick.

The shape was somewhat crude—oh, well,
Something like a cockleshell;
The strings across the misshaped hole,
Gave the thing a bit more soul.
And on each end of this contraption,
A rope strap—for authentication—
Hung to emphasize the whole,
And the music of his soul.
No need for stagefright in this setting,
Or the worry of forgetting.

The first phrase came with confidence,
Loud and clear he sang the cadence.
It was "I'm looking over,"
A pause, "a four-leaf clover."
Then sucking in more oxygen,
He sang the first line once again.
It was hard to know if he,
Had repeated purposely;
Or if his memory missed a beat,
With his little sneakered feet.

His fingers flew across the strings,
Birdlike, but with slower wings.
Sharps or flats he did not know,
Or the word "adagio,"
But he sang on with social ease,
Only with intent to please,
"That I overlooked before."
Here he checked his music score,

Then he got a bit more bold,
And slipped in a full beat hold,
Messing up the four-four beat
As words poured out across my feet.
He tried hard to be a pro,
With voice pitched high and then quite low.
"No need esplaining," the "x"
Was not so clear, and then the apex
Sung louder, "It's somebody I adore,"
So cute this little troubadour.

And on and on he went forgetting,
He was in a temporal setting;
I never knew if he did finish,
But the thought I'll always cherish,
And for all that I might know,
He could still be carrying on the show.

The Weatherman

He said tonight 'twould be quite cold,
　　Hovering near the twenty mark,
I covered up the marigolds,
　　Even in the doggone dark.

He also said the wind would blow
　　And showed the fronts upon the screen,
He pointed where the lines would go,
　　And where the rain would fall, 'twas green.

They gave him extra time to show this,
　　Because a snowstorm was a-comin',
It seemed so sure he couldn't miss,
　　I grabbed the lawn chairs, brought 'em in.

He proudly showed the doppler radar,
　　With the ripples runnin' through,
It sounded like a candy bar,
　　But it was science, and quite new.

I left my knitting and the yarn,
　　Lying tangled in the chair,
Then hurricd out to check the barn,
　　With a blanket for the mare.

And wouldn't ya know, the door got stuck,
　　It come right off the upper hinge,
I propped it up with a hockey puck,
　　Took twenty minutes, it made me cringe.

So back to the big old house I flew,
    And hurried to shut the bedroom window,
The one where the wind and rain came through,
    Then tossed on the bed a knitted throw.

I looked all over for the weather-stripping,
    But couldn't find it, or there was no more.
And by that time the eaves were dripping,
    And I dragged myself to lock the door.

I crawled in bed with a quilt to my neck,
    And those ugly booties on my feet,
Who cared how I looked, so what the heck,
    No one could see 'em under the sheet.

I slept so good that night until
    The alarm went off with a shocking blast,
It was time to take my one last pill;
    But the morning news left me aghast.

There had been no storm and wouldn't be,
    Again the weatherman was wrong;
A farmer had more sense than he,
    If he looked at clouds and sky for long.

My Casa Guidi Windows

My "Casa Guidi Windows" cannot boast the pageantry,
That passed the Florence windows, so long ago in Italy;
  Mine, closer to the rural setting than one so much
    alive,
  And has a name that sounds impressive, though it's
    just a drive.

I do not have a Grand Duke, in a carriage fine and
    grand,
Passing with his retinue, followed by a band;
  I only see some children playing on a grassy hill,
  And in winter watch them sledding to get a winter
    thrill.

I do not hear some child's sweet voice singing "Liberty"
As when Italy weighed her strength and fought so
    valiantly.
  I only hear the screech of sirens, and see a flashing
    light,
  Wondering where the trouble is on such a chilly
    night.

There is no crowd of soldiers dancing in the cobbled
    street
With a lady, celebrating victory with their feet.
  I only have the quiet weeks with business and some
    pleasure,
  And seek other places to enjoy the music's measure.

There is no cathedral, just across a cobbled way,
Where people join together for a marriage or to pray;
   But we have a steady flow every morn and evening,
As people drive away to whatever they're achieving.

The Arno, like a silvery ribbon sheen with its flow
Underneath the ancient bridges, from the Florence
      window,
   Has only a small replica below my balcony,
   But my rivulet has given equal pleasure to me.

It is less than a stone's throw across my narrow stream,
And so shaded that it cannot give that silvery gleam.
   If I could, I'm not sure I'd change the scenery,
   Because you see, my love extends to friend and
      family.

What need have I of Florence or Dante sitting in a
      square?
There is enough for me to watch on my own
      thoroughfare.
So I will leave the Florence picture in the books I've
      read,
To tease another writer to say the things I've left unsaid.

Let This Cup Pass from Me

" . . . Let this cup pass from me . . . ,"
It was what our Lord did say
   In Gethsemane,
   When he knelt alone to pray;
But the prayer that followed was not heard,
   As on His brow stood drops of sweat and blood,
   But a keen apocalyptic thud
Rolled down the centuries, where they were sepulchred
   in the hearts of those,
   Where a caring spirit blows.
Could it be those drops of blood prefigured
   Other drops from thorns at Calvary,
   Or the dark night in Hades' agony
After earthly flesh had been interred?
   And now our human cries,
   With Jesus' words amalgamize.

   Let this cup pass from me
Of the pain that is my lot,
   It is not destiny,
   Only that which was ill-got;
Take from me all discomfort, fever flush,
   Or let my spirit soar above the moan,
   And press the prayer full out above the groan,
That steals its way into the night's deep hush.
   Hear now this penitent,
   And crush the lispings of lament.

Let this cup pass from me,
Of the disappointment stirring
   A dust to discontent,
Lest I host the entering
Of demons waiting at the threshold,
   To slip their unforgiving spirits in,
   And the fault of others enlarge my sin,
Until my own fault multiplies fourfold;
     Let not this little thing
   Be the clouding of my life-spring.

Let this cup pass from me
Of the hate that gathers 'round
   Breeding infamy;
Instead let floods of love abound,
That the raging nations may be healed;
   And drown the will of tyrants in a sea
   Of altar fires burning steadily,
Until our knees have every wrong repealed,
     That perplex our nation,
   And shroud the truth in disputation.

Let this cup pass from me,
Of the newcasts droning on
   A dreary litany,
Repeating like a marathon
The child abuses, shattering childish trust
   (Like the careless footsteps on the tender
   Reeds before the growth comes tall and slender)
That dulls their sparkling eyes once filled with stardust;
     Meant to shine out glories,
   From the courts of paradise.

Let this cup pass from me,
   Of the unkind words I heard today,
      Let them pass and hurry,
      Into hollows of decay;
Like the dead leaves pressed into the ground,
      Waiting for the mottled heap to mellow,
      And be mixed with elements that follow
Nature's inclinations in their round,
         Then waking to new beauty,
         From their bosomed reverie.

      Let this cup pass from me,
   Of the leaden sorrow folding close
      Around a memory,
      That all my senses now engross;
The wound once-buried deep beneath the scar.
      O years, O time, returning for redress
      To melt away a long, long loneliness,
Make this open heart progenitor
         For a brighter future,
         And swallow up the bitter myrrh.

      Let this cup pass from me?
   I would not let it pass for naught;
      But sip the bitter alocs fully,
      'Til the nectar I have sought,
Turns the bitter dregs to honey-sweet.
         For if I thwart life's stormy diapason,
         Might I not also miss the antiphon,
Sealed in the capsule of the bitter sweet?
         "Not my will but thine . . . "
         Shall be spoken at my shrine;
For in His will the whole world He may bless,
         While my will may miss or overreach,

Or omit a point that I should teach.
Where this finite being can only guess,
        Seems a counterfeit,
        Measured 'gainst the infinite.

Flying

Ah, the thrill to be able to fly,
    To be the envy of all below,
To soar like a bird through the deep blue sky,
    Only to be grounded by pure white snow.

To be free from the burdens of others,
    While mere mortals gaze up in awe,
To do stunts as thrilling as any others,
    And people say, "Did you see what I saw?"

To be where no man can touch me,
    Where the sky and the earth are my friend,
To be above the world where I'm free,
    Where the paths I can fly have no end.
(This poem was written by the author's son, Calvin
    Ward, and included in this book by his permission.)

Luke

Before me now those laughing impish eyes,
    Are slipping through the shiny photo glaze
To study if my thoughts run contrariwise
    To yours, or if you look for some small praise.

Adorable that little rounded face,
    With a smile that jumps out from the frame;
But that picture ne'er can take the place,
    Of hands and feet that quicken to a game.

Nor can your cheek absorb the warmth of heart,
    In spite of all the times I press your head
Behind the glass, it misses that warm dart;
    I'd rather put the kiss upon your flesh instead.

It would be fun to see and hear you play,
    Even though the jabber be outrageous
To one who is now old and mostly gray,
    No longer seeking to be emulous.

But now I must content myself to gaze
    Upon your picture with heart standing by,
And hope there will not be too many days,
    Before we see each other eye to eye.

Tucker

Sleep, sleep on, your life has just begun,
Wake, but not too quickly, sleeping one,
    We would not have you miss an angel kiss,
Nor have that angel leave her work undone.

Your mother has left off her lullaby,
When she sensed an angel hovering nigh.
    To take up the strain of her refrain,
Then left the angel heart to sanctify.

Here and there you stole a slanted peek,
As if to play a game of hide-and-seek;
    With a new world pressing on your guessing,
While you stored visions just above your cheek.

And those tiny hands that had no aim,
Turned quickly to a solitary game,
    For your own amusing and future using,
'Til strengthened so, they'll one day write your name.

Those tiny hands now busy as a flitting bee
Are prodded by a curiosity;
    To hold a newfound treasure, for a measure,
Then release it with dexterity.

Those "oohs" and "ahs" and verbal utterances,
Are responded to with sweet pretenses;
    Heaven only knows, the thoughts you chose,
So heaven alone must know their inferences.

Then came those first two steps to round the year,
While eagerly all watched to give you cheer;
    And waited patient for that first encore,
To seal the first one with a strength that's clear.

With attainment in your baby art,
You've wrapped us step by step around your heart
    With fun and laughter, and hereafter
We will take up each blessing you impart.

On the Passing of Norman

Rest now, rest now, brother dear,
    The rest that was your own soul's yearning,
But let me lean a little near,
    Before much time may dull my burning,

If indeed it could be dulled,
    with such a poignant past to swell
The memory, so chronicled
    In the mind's small citadel.

Listen now for my heart strain,
    Laying words upon your soul,
With pressures spirits ascertain,
    Reaching heavenward roll on roll.

I saw your weakness creeping steady,
    Like the vanishing of day,
Gliding slowly into night,
    That my heart could not gainsay.

I remember when they called you
    "Sunshine," as a little child,
Or was it just a sweet response,
    To attentions kind and mild?

You tried so hard with little strength,
    To always do the manly thing,
Though tiring in two hours' length,
    Before I wished to end our outing.

I pondered on the stalking giant,
    Sapping life before my eyes,
So relentless and defiant,
    Refusing to rejuvenize.

When I prayed for life, the fear
    Of death stalked through my very being,
And tainted that small ounce of cheer,
    That made my prayer more unbelieving.

How I longed to do more, give more.
    Counting it a little thing,
Knowing you might leave this shore,
    And soon my heart would feel the death-sting.

Yet with all that purple presence,
    Filtering through our thought and word,
We dared not speak the plainer essence,
    That hovering angels must have heard.

Too close those angels were for comfort,
    But then, they had a work to do;
Soon all our visits were cut short,
    Because your time had come for you.

Too soon it came, you just lay down,
    Like it was something that you meant
To do, giving up the earthly crown
    Of life, for one more permanent.

The Memory of Trudy

Can I say I miss you, friend
    When we lived so far apart?
For well the world might so contend,
    But they cannot see my heart.

When first we met I could not waver
    In my thought, that we would be
Friends forever, and I still savor
    The touch that fell so mystically.

The time and distance never caused
    An awkward moment from one parting.
To the next encounter, just paused,
    To let our thought take wing.

Your patient ear and understanding,
    Gave me a place to rest upon.
You listened to my chattering
    In a wordy marathon.

Our spirit hearts met with one goal,
    And into common thought they pressed,
As though we wrote the selfsame scroll,
    And each aimed for the selfsame quest.

Time has passed since you left
    This world, and all your many cares,
And now there is a little cleft,
    That I have filled with thoughts and prayers.

Tristan da Cunha

This poem was created out of a documentary film seen on the PBS channel. The utter remoteness of this small island in the middle of the South Pacific Ocean is seen in its people who are maintained by the British. It is believed that at one time someone had been shipwrecked there. They were not the usual uncivilized natives that one encounters in such remote parts, but were completely alone without the heterogeneous elements surrounding most communities. One got the impression that they did not know how to interact with strangers and preferred to remain aloof.

1

Tristan da Cunha, so alone and so remote,
    Like an exile on a sea of green;
From a distance seemed to bob and float,
    At the point where sea and land convene.

2

Tristan da Cunha, slips easily from the lips,
    And catches up the mind into a vision,
Then holds it fast within a mystic grip,
    Not knowing how it made the smooth transition.

3

Were these the tricks played by uncertainty,
    Or apprehension with its swaying mood;
Half from fear and half from ecstasy,
    Seeking answers in the solitude?

4

Would the stranger have a joyous welcome?
    How would he greet them if it were not so?
His spirit mixed with the noisy tedium,
    Of waves rising high, then sinking low.

5

Could this isle be a jewel of England's crown?
    Who knows? But from it what would be the gain?
There's little trade to swell the isle's renown,
    Lying stultified like some brown stain,

6

Floating on that broad expanse of seas.
    And now a single ship six times a year,
Does battle with the helmsman and the breeze,
    Half in hopefulness and half in fear.

7

With such relentless splash and leaping, island
    Boats are hoisted from their habitat
Onto land for calmer, safer keeping,
    From out the hostile waves playing autocrat.

8

Tristan ever witnessing wild motion,
    Stands stiff and dauntless in the interplay,
Like a cradle in the midst of ocean,
    Sitting in the middle of harm's way.

9

What is this fascination with wild beauty,
    That slips o'er danger as it were a word
Upon a page, or necessary duty,
    As though the threat of danger were absurd?

10

And rising on the northmost shore, a silent
    Menace lifts its head into the blue,
Like some high potentate of parliament
    Robed in emerald green to help the view,

11

Maintaining aspects of a status quo,
    In muted attestation base to peak,
Brooding o'er the simple life below,
    While listening for the thundergod to speak.

12

And speak it has with all the furry rumbling
    From its bosom like a demagogue,
Boldly flashing edicts in the thundering,
    Like last impressions in an epilogue.

13

The isle itself is no metropolis,
    With only one dwarfed steeple to expose it;
No flashing neon lights or frenzied commerce
    To wake it from the stillness of its spirit.

14

What sins retained? What lack of lavishment,
    Without an airstrip and no easy course,
To beat a path to civil enfranchisement
    That other lands so readily endorse.

15

At last down dropt the boat to ferry guests,
    Eager for a welcome sign from shore,
But only two men sat like stone on stone
    Unmoved—or so it seemed—but nothing more.

16

Overhead the pure white albatross
    Dipt and flapped their narrow wings along
The margin of the bayless shore, to cross
    And recross, writing out their welcome song,

17

The only sign the crew and guests received.
    No sound of mirth or curiosity
Was evoked, nor was there one perceived,
    And none stepped forth to fake a curtsy.

18

To what frame of mind will such reaction
    Mold a people into orthodoxy,
Without a touch of heartfelt adulation,
    To spin the wheels out of monotony?

19

Where the smile that links a soul with soul,
    To make a sunny path from light to light?
This would seem to be the natural goal,
    And give to each a boon of sweet delight.

20

Where the children who do make events,
    Of little things and stir an apathy,
Then drop the sunshine down with no pretense,
    To add a gloss to dull propriety?

21

And where the maiden girls who come to gaze
    Into a stranger's face and find in it
The same thoughts that they entertain, then raise
    Their eyes to meet his, just for the fun of it?

22

Where the handshake? Where the sparkling eye
    That opens up to let the stranger in,
Or any other sign to edify
    Each with some gesture a little genuine?

23

It is stated in that Book eternal,
    To entertain the stranger at the door,
To make our Christian claim effectual,
    For angels unawares may be that visitor.

24

Etched on stones were seven family names,
    Mixing with the wildflowers on the slope,
One German and the rest spelled Scotch and Irish,
    All linked now in broader faith and scope.

25

Here seven family names for seven miles
    Leave little room for major complications,
And less to battle with where less defiles,
    But narrows space for greater aspirations.

26

All nature's here, tilt to contempt or scorn,
    Toward those who are more enterprising men;
And attitudes like sacraments are worn,
    As the garments of the Saracen.

27

Life that stirs upon this shore seems forged
    Into some pattern of utopia,
But waits upon a larger heart to merge
    The form with a more joyful replica.

28

With a single preacher to expound
    The truths both esoteric and the evident,
Who to challenge should they not be sound?
    Or give depth to concept and the sacrament?

29

What infraction of a muted code
    Divided church pews into "Men" and "Women?"
Their departures following the same mode,
    Made one wonder how they entered in.

30

As the organ played the last, amen,
    In single file the ladies made their exit,
Followed by the suit-and-tie clad men;
    No preacher at the door with word or wit,

31

To take a lonely hand in a warm clasp,
    And by a touch perform a miracle.
And no children reaching for the grasp,
    Just to learn a simple ritual.

32

No room here for a competitor
    With just one teacher and one current text,
Where lies the student challenge to explore,
    A broader spectrum of a single concept?

33

Who's to call their mentor right or wrong,
    He just *is,* and every child he teaches
Has his stamp upon him, weak or strong,
    And if you know but one, you know what each is.

34

There's little to disturb this island peace,
    As days unfold into the common things,
And weeks pass slowly for the year's increase,
    And for winters sliding into springs.

35

There's fishing, cows, and planting, even stamps,
    To fill the time and seasons as they pass,
And knitted woolen socks to keep the damps
    From feet, still seasoned to the summer grass.

36

Yet some have stepped into another mold,
    No question that the vision stretched afar,
And with a thrust that ranks them with the bold,
    They sought out other places, other stars.

37

From whence did some wind blow across the deep
    To leave a human print upon this shore?
Was it a dream to fill a restless sleep,
    Or reading of *Utopia* by More?

38

It matters not if shipwrecked or intended,
    Or exiled from a scene more politic,
Where one's reason loomed, yet undefended
    Because of some unwitting rhetoric,

39

The seed was planted, and now the British crown,
    Nourishes it with books and bikes and stamps,
With organs, clothes and tools to build their town,
    Sitting on the edge of dews and damps.

40

Another ship arrives, another crew,
    Perhaps another preacher and some guest
And a small band of just a meager few,
    To sing and play rock music. "I make no jest."

41

The time had come for the departure,
    And the stranger felt an alien still;
No more the island held such keen allure,
    No more he held the passion in his will.

42

On the shore he stood once more alone,
    Listening to the ship's strong grinding wheel,
Chugging out a saddened undertone,
    Breaking bands that triggered the appeal.

Elysian Fields

Part 1. The Struggle

The last of summer's glorious tints had slipped
    Her colors into autumn's golden flush;
Before her own buds could be fully nipped,
    She sought to hold in check the fuller blush.
The sun, now moving to its destined height,
    Was unwilling to concede her shine
To chills that drove her beauty to a blight,
    With swift strokes to hasten her decline.

The willow's crispy greens hung draped about,
    Encircling like an aura all who sat
Beneath the shade—the ribald and devout—
    To serve as temporary habitat.
Thus sat a poet searching for a line
    To draw upon the world's broad windowpane,
A mural with a gem in its design,
    In hopes of lessening all the sordid strain.

With his pen poised for the alchemy,
    He searched hard for words to mark the beat;
Now wont to fingering meters on his knee,
    Refused to make the rhythm all complete.
The stream beside him murmured senseless babble,
    Fearful lest an icy crest might seal her tongue.
Mindness it flowed o'er every obstacle,
    To where the pepper-red of sumac hung,

To mock his spirit with her spicy leaf.
　　The nettle, dried and blown, but who knew where?
At least without her pricks was some relief.
　　Daisies stood with chilled and soulless glare,
No wonder when their future seemed so grim.
　　Even latticed shade dropped like a pall,
And dangled like a paper ghost about him,
　　And all, all filled with empty ritual.

Straining at a hope for consonance,
　　Was not the stuff of which to form an art;
Too much the senses were at variance,
　　That kept all thoughts and senses far apart,
Until he cried, "Cursed or benign these thoughts
　　That rise like missile-heads, then overrun
Their mark, out of purpose, out of sight,
　　Or to archives of oblivion.

"If I evoke a prayer then doubt its worth,
　　(The very meat that is prerequisite,
That angels need to bring it into birth)
　　'Twould cancel out the very fruit of it.
Jacob on his desert stone entreated
　　Boldly for a blessing to descend;
Though my prayers touch not the mercy seat,
　　I will cling as he, to find *my* end."

Sol, crept slowly to his appointed place,
　　Hazed all the ethers 'round, a paler hue;
Clouds below seemed more than commonplace,
　　Like steps, one on one, and not a few,
Dropping steadily down from an aperture,
　　Top to base, it was phenomenal!
Perhaps the sylphs were seeking some new venture
　　To adumbrate a scene more mystical.

136

Still eager to engage his pen than stay
   Upon cloud capers he could not explain,
He soon forgot the mystical display,
   Seen through the branching of the tree's domain.
Nestled in between two roots for comfort
   He recalled some long-forgotten lines,
That were simple, childlike, and made in sport.
   Verse created 'mong the forest pines.

    "Nature lends herself most freely
      To the poet's clever rhyme,
    And is more the able maestro,
      To beat out the proper time.
    Her moods and colors all provide,
      A wardrobe for poetic dress,
    Comforts rather than to chide,
      And leave a poet in distress."

Oft bards did make a Merlin's chair of stone,
   And sing their songs in praise of heedless creatures,
Or feel the pulse and passion of a throne,
   Molding with a pen the nation's features.
And other flights into the soul of things
   Mount high, then fall softly on a page,
To make a mark with literary wings,
   And hailing him a prophet of the age.

Such pondering freed his mind and spirit too,
   Releasing a fresh flow through every nerve
And drew his heart and will to now renew
   His aim and purpose, with a steady verve.
His eyes now focused on the knoll across
   The stream, were fastened too upon a glow,

And shimmering at the heart, a cross,
    Like a prelude for celestial show.

It quickened all his senses to a splendor,
    That enwrapped him like a silken cloak;
There was naught he could do but surrender
    To the peace that fell so like a stroke.
And just as suddenly a light broke forth,
    That filled the space where once the steps had been
And transformed the knoll to sacred altar,
    Without the serving angels being seen.

Amidst the circling spirals there appeared
    A form, in blue arrayed. You could not tell
Whether form itself had been ensphered,
    Or the sphere the form's own parallel,
So ensconced he was in golden glory,
    Poised on the spot the cherubim had made,
Preparing for some heavenly oratory.
    As a Greek god on high. With eyes deep-laid

Looked clear into the poet's wonderment;
    There could be no mistake, if you read
His eyes, you also read God's testament.
    (Such knowing could make one disquieted).
In the silence you thought his silence spoke.
    He looked not right nor left, he had one goal
In view, to enhance all poets' worth:
    The silence now, a muted thunder-roll.

One gesture made he with his outstretched hand
    And beckoned, *that* His only inference,
His grace and manner were a clear command,
    There was no need to doubt such competence.

They passed unnoticed through the mortal veil
  To worlds of other knowing, other sight,
Leaving not as much as one thin trail,
  To mark the destination of their flight.

Interlude

Before them was a temple high and grand,
  More majestic than human mind could fathom,
Who could craft such art with human hand,
  Lest some artist tapped a greater wisdom.

Huge doors embellished in bold arabesque
  With ivory carvings, were a master's art,
And interspersed with ancient romanesque;
  In all of sculpture there was no counterpart.

The holy, holy, holy, that outpoured
  From the flaming altar endlessly,
Though sweetly sung a thousand times and more,
  Still repeated it adoringly.

Beyond the confines of the sanctuary,
  Spread a grand and endless scene, all open
As earth's sky had been, and very airy,
  With here and there a stream, a hill, a glen.

Part II. The Pool of Tears

A violet pool swelled thrice, no more,
But no display disturbed the shore;
  Much like a maiden standing still

May heave her breast when love does injure,
Or some fond glance lodge deep within her
    For remembering at her will.

The waters to the depth reflected
All about, and naught rejected.
    Pink clouds with soft intensity,
Formed their fleecy continents,
That in the pool made deep imprints,
    By sylphs that labored patiently.

In the midst the angel stood
Upon a mist as angel could,
    And with her presence poet claimed.
Her silent gaze alone commanded,
Naught praised, and naught she reprimanded,
    But from her being a sweetness reigned.

Virtues spread their radiance,
To ornament her countenance,
    Golden framed and ample tressed.
Her gown soft-hued in violet dyes,
Deepened the purple of her eyes.
    And with them poet was twice blessed.

Her feet as white-formed alabaster,
Was of her poise the perfect master,
    Like a sculptured pedestal.
If lilies bloomed where now the mist,
Discerning eyes might also guess,
    The flower too incorporeal

Her hands in mercy oils deep-washed,
Gave healing in their airy touch,
　　Pale-pinked with life and delicate;
They seemed as rosebuds on a stem,
Awaiting countless bees to kiss them
　　And a thousand sweets beget.

"These, my son" (her gesture flowed
As though her whole being were an ode,
　　And with his being was interfused)
"Are the tears that men have shed,
That are by listening angels read
　　To test them for their motive used.

"No anguished tear is here contained,
That is not first by heaven strained,
　　To cleanse it lest it vitiate;
Contrition must the anguish bleed,
That gnaws on fear or foul misdeed,
　　They make the drop invalidate.

"Sorrow too may leave a taint,
If tongue shall wrap it in complaint,
　　Such make the tear less virtuous,
And the intended fruit undo;
These shall need another to
　　Provide a layer for the dross."

Here she paused in pensive mood,
And in that poignant interlude,
　　Pricked the poet's memory,
For anguish once his soul had rent,
And burning robbed it of content,
　　Where once blossomed harmony.

At the moment of the prick,
A light upon his dark shone quick,
   Like night hit sudden by the sun;
Seeing with a new soul sight,
He was willing to requite,
   Unholy deeds that he had done.

Lest he should on that anguish stay,
Made she haste to blot away
   The sting that furrowed his low brow.
(He thought he heard a sweet bird's song
Riding zephyrs, carrying it along)
   His head bent low in prayer to vow.

Again the angel bending, mute,
Gently touched his heart to suit
   A proper joy to match his need,
And with a smile he understood,
She blessed him well as angel would,
   And then gave one more word, "Godspeed."

Part III. The Knights

The willing guide responded to the word,
"Godspeed," as though it were an impulse heard,
And by the infinite had been inured.

So deftly was the changing of the scene,
With not a flutter made in the routine,
Unlike the clatter heard behind a screen

When it drops adown that silken door,
Secluding audience from troubadour.
In that round hall of noble knights, the floor

Emitted ever a soft shimmering glow,
Matching pulse for pulse, the very low
Playing of an oratorio.

Twelve pedestals—fine-formed—of polished beryl,
Each with a sculptured scroll outlined in pearl,
Had a name carved in the sweeping curl.

Twelve images of brave and noble knight,
Topped each column like an acolyte,
Shining twice the brilliance in sunlight.

All devout and poised like minute men,
Exuding strength of an Olympian,
So perfect was the hand of artisan,

You could not guess if stone or flesh stood by.
One pure knight with lance and still-set eye,
Had fixed a goal, firm too that hefty thigh;

Made stout and strong from all the jousts he played,
And all the battles fought so unafraid,
Yet not one whispered word of his crusade.

But one there was, the priest, Sir Percivale,
Who spoke of Galahad in Arthur's hall,
That sealed his vow when the light broke mystical,

In a glory covering Merlin's chair,
That stretched up castle walls in holy glare,
Sending flaming tongues into the air.

On a shield marked plain and ivy-clad,
A motet blazed in praise of Galahad,
And through it flowed the balm of Gilead.

Young voices sang the motet soft and clear,
Breathing words into the atmosphere,
Devout mixed with a touch of holy cheer.

The Motet

To Galahad of Arthur's hall
This tribute shall forever be,
An accolade most admirable,
To his selfless constancy.

His life a silent paragon
Of vigilance and chastity,
Ensconced his virtues into one,
A robe of pure humility.

Whose wrappings have concealed each deed,
Despising trophies of display,
Heaven alone his love, his creed,
The Holy Grail his goal, his way.

His loyalty to king and vows,
Not lightly ta'en upon his knee,
Bound him to the cause he espoused,
And by that binding set him free.

144

And ever will his name preserve
The thought of nobleness in man,
Awakening the virtuous nerve,
From king to proletarian.

The Second Knight

One knight appeared to leap from his high stance,
like a dedicated warrior, intent
upon the battle and the victory.
A vigilance evinced in every line
of the majestic brow was furrowed with
high thought and purpose. Michelangelo,
could not shape plainer strength of form and limb
than this great artisan evoked, a moving,
thinking being within his knife. If blood
and nerve flowed through this stone you could not sense
a presence clearer, ready to break forth
from form to life. 'Twas like a touch from other
worlds sliding down to mark the finite
with impressions infinite. No pilgrim
could resist the drawing of the deep-set
eyes with such intensity of purpose,
that followed where you moved, and yet gazed conscious,
far adown God's great infinity,
where past and future met and synthesized.
His lips set perfectly above his jaw,
—Though barely parted—spoke clear influences,
in silences that no one could refute.

145

A sudden sound as of a rushing wind,
followed by six brassy trumpets, blasted
unfamiliar notes into their ears
and stunned them rudely back into the present,
much like an unexpected storm will stir
the dust of plains that have lain too long
in an August sun. All eyes were drawn
to six archangels emerging like a vision
from the "Isle of Patmos" to trumpet judgments,
came instead in praise of this bold knight.
The brilliance of their rainment compelled
each eyelid downward, as a child devout,
just off from play, would abruptly come
upon a sacrament and quickly seek a cleansing,
from an unknown sin should there be any.
With eyes now lowered, each saw emblazoned in
the sweeping curl the name of, St. Germain,
And in prophetic tones heard of his mission:
"Freedom for a planet is his cause."

Here each bard's thoughts wandered much at will,
reflecting on some phase almost forgotten.
Some thought on freedom, many thought on love.
Some, how to govern justly and with mercy.
Others—in more humble state—thought only
how best to implement the golden rule.
One poet thought of beauty, the same who sat
distraught beside the stream seeking words
and inspiration, but now suddenly
became aware that beauty must have depth
and height to impel it on to greater
uses, lest it stagnate in the moment.
Though beauty be an abstract thing it needs
the pulse of human heart to expand . . .

His thoughts broke quickly into words leaving
half the sound upon his lips and half
to sink into his soul.

The sights of beauty
may impress upon the mind awareness
of it, but appreciation gives
the thrust to drive it deeper, and weave it gently
into noble uses. One muse so aptly
stated, " . . . Beauty in the mind leaves
the hearth cold . . . " It was clear that inspiration
was the spice to consummate the fruit.

Each guarded his own revelation as though
he had found the pearl of greatest price.
In this there was a bonding of their spirits,
preparing them for unspeakable delight.

Soft cadences outflowed upon the ethers,
beating in three-quarter time, that came
from every point, or no point at all;
and keeping with the beat, a spectrum grand.
A kaleidoscope of color, outburst a golden
chalice, like streamers weaving in, then out,
and on the end of each a dancer costumed
in the color most suited to herself.
The gasp now heard—the only sound intruding
on the silence—was as it were one breath;
and those who would speak words for the beauty
of it, could not utter them. They glided
graceful without fault to the strains
of "Vienna Woods," in such a soundless
mode it made the perfect pantomime.

One dancer robed in pastel blue looked most
familiar to the struggling poet—as those
who view are wont to do—and on her he kept
a steadfast gaze, lost in wondrous beauty.
Among the bards there was no consciousness
of aught save sheer delight of uninterrupted
reverie, that seemed more like a dream
than anything so real. Then slowly gliding
out of view they made their noiseless exit.

When the last measures had lost their pulse,
    In long dulcet tones trailing away,
Left was the throb and a strong impulse,
    To carry the tune to a holiday.

Then a joy struck through to the earth below
    That inspired a song that a patriot sang,
It lifted a sorrow and calmed a foe,
    And on and on it rang and rang.

No one could guess from whence it came,
    But a listening angel caught the thrill,
And repeated the song in his own domain,
    Then passed it along to the stars until

It returned to the place of origin,
    To the very spot where the knights had been,
But instead of the knights a gate therein,
    Very high-arched and opaline.

Part IV. The Temple

Beyond the arch a portico rose grandly,
with eight white giant marble columns pressing
pastel patterns through the opaque stone.
And arching round the base were fern—the airy
kind—and at each top the fleur-de-lis
displayed a tripart plume in colors three,
hewn faultlessly beneath blue granite glaze
of roof. Each plume was knotted with a pearl
so large, that one might think it was more common
to a nautilus shell than like the usual
jewel. Atop the dome a steeple pierced
the sky, but one could not discern the reach,
but you might guess it did extend to endless
rims of cosmic space. Stiff guards stood ready
with their lances as praetorian guards
would defend against intruders at
an emperor's palace gate. It was easy
to assume that they were chosen for
their eager willingness to keep pure
the way of truth. Too numerous the guards
to keep a steady eye upon them in a
faultless count, but it was duly noted
their faithful diligence and constancy.

The impressive scene evoked their spirits
to evaluate their faithfulness.
With their minds now quickened one thought prevailed,
*Where light is given there falls upon a man
responsibility.* Each felt a cloak
of density surround their auras and knew
it for the burden of illumination,
and entered reverently into the temple.

149

One being alone stood on the pearly dais,
so radiant you lost the sight of form,
but you could not miss the emanations
of an ancient wisdom descending without
pauses. Precise and clear the tones dropped down
as pebbles do into caverns of the
deep. It made one wonder if their quiet
depth recorded its decibels:
for you could not see this patriarch's
lips nor see his face, or you lost
the sound in the vastness of the place.

His opening remarks began with, "Greetings,"
and then a reverence fell quite suddenly,
drawing each one into rapt attention.
He began his discourse with a statement
that fell profoundly on each poet present.

"Here all truth is predicated on
the law of love and cannot be disputed,"
The thought and feeling riveted to depths
heretofore not known or felt by any.
The muses sat transfixed and lived wholly
in this eternal moment, not wanting to
pass on to other thought for fear they lose
the impact of his words.

But all transcending
moments pass and gently drop one into
slots of time, yet leaving memory
to prod us onward to our destinies.
With mild gestures the ancient sage continued.
"In this dimension there is no need for words,

for words are symbols, nor can words feed thought,
lest law itself become contaminated.
Here avarice or hate can never spread
their tentacles, for in this peaceful clime
love is ever constant and serene."

One bard struggled inwardly with how
to put pure love to words. How could he translate
such a concept into earthly symbols?
Even Dante could not adequately
define his Beatrice, though he press her into
every page, in spite of all the darkness,
that surrounded that blest soul of light.
He found himself again, the poet struggling
to hold fast the master's precept given.
The mentor once again resumed his discourse,
This time without a recognition of
the silence following it, for thought transcended
thought as one would leave a lesser chore
to fill a greater need.
Much like a maestro's
pause before he gives his orchestra
the cue for the final measure, he spoke:
"Dear muses, your art with poet-colored phrases,
with similes and metaphors fashioning
windows to let your light of wisdom through,
have done much to stir the hearth fires with
your grains of truth, but now a higher law
attends you to transcend your former work
and for this purpose we have summoned you."

All felt this master gave bold utterance
with prophetic knowing, seeing endings
from beginnings, and speaking only that

which could produce the greatest good. He drew
them as a prophet would for a special
revelation, to give some clarity
to chaos, or to verify a whim.

"Causes and effects are woven through
philosophies both ancient and in modern
texts, but causes often are evasive,
for time builds bridges slowly to effects,
making their beginnings much obscured.
Bane and blessing weave their episodes
twixt birth and death, but little known are those
that quicken life beyond the human realm."

Here this patriarch now paused to give
each guest a time to ponder on his words,
for some there were who had not thought upon
the concept of a never-ending life.
No one present had desire to probe
into focus, past episodes to test
the master's words, but yielded to his own soul's
revelations, and for the first time felt
alone in this great temple of God's wisdom.

Some recalled a moment when they pondered
justice. It was evident that this wise
guru followed all their mental wanderings
and fit his words into their thoughts: "Where was
justice when one seemed free of consequences
of gross sin, while another suffered
silent or with moaning for the causes
that should have been the first man's fate? And what
of seeds we plant of thoughts and deeds producing
in like kind as fruit unto the tree?

Would God unjustly give to one that which
is another's lot, invalidate
His established law and make Himself
unjust? If this were so, what chaos might
ensue throughout our worlds and galaxies?
Who could then have faith in God, if God
lack justice? Would each man then proclaim himself
a God? Could the effect be anarchy?"
Those who thought upon his words seemed drawn
to a past, familiar but remote.

Another bard was most intense in his
reverie, for he saw himself
upon a screen as a begging child
with his bowl, among the rubble where
lepers kept a bit of fire burning.
Few there were to pass, and few took pity.
Those who looked upon him with compassion
paused to pray then passed to other duties.

But one there was who beckoned him as though
he wished to speak or aid him secretly.
He saw the grateful tears drop down the young
but pallid cheek—not yet fully shaped
to maturity—and felt the kinship
stirring deep within him. His spirit lightened
when he noted an approaching angel,
hastening to absorb the tear trickling
from the child's soft eye, and with her wing-tips
dried it smooth from off his hollowed cheek.

A second scene appeared beside the first.
This one of a young and robust man
looking like the twin of his own self,
living in an opulence that could
befit a prince, laughing, reckless with his
life and means, and thoughtless of the waifs
about him, (who themselves could only wish
to emulate his deeds) saw where these
acts had carved his future. An overwhelming
gratitude o'ertook him for forgiveness
given, that effected a sure healing.
The scene then slowly vanished.

Other bards
More meditative, had varying revelations;
cognizant of a link from life to life,
showing a long sequence now unfolding.
This group was more profound and radiated
greater wisdom; but their guard was more
intense, for pride could easily replace
humility.

Dispersed among this temple
gathering were neophytes selected merely
to observe. The presiding master
was most careful with these little lambs,
for he discerned among them those prone to doubt
so did not press them, but only waited eager
for their souls to gather in more light.
He then spoke briefly, admonishing, "Sweet singers,
of the earth remember, where light is given
there falls upon a man responsibility."
All here were given pause to readjust
the depth of their own natures and felt

themselves drawn closer to the throne of truth.
The sage then raised his arms in benediction
and all passed contemplatively into
the children's bower.

Part V. The Children's Bower

Yellows by some alchemy were pinked,
   Meadow beauties turned to violet hue,
You could declare that all the flowers winked,
   But it was rainbows sparkling through the dew.

Honeysuckle made their speedy climb,
   To top a latticed trellis, a wonder too,
The trellis looked like fragile gossamer,
   And flowers played a game of peek-a-boo.

Elves and cherubs circled in and out,
   Weaving ribbons through the columbine;
It looked for all the world the thing throughout,
   Was in the making for a valentine.

Whether valentine or miracle,
   As your several fancy may befit,
The whole performance was so comical,
   You smiled, or laughed out for the fun of it.

The birdlike columbine outdid its size,
   To match the head and wingspan of the bird,
And the littlest cherubs offered a surprise
   By sliding down the ribbons, then subtly lured

The elementals to their antic fun,
    And jettisoned to ground with lightning speed,
To the wondering eyes of everyone,
    Unmindful cherubs did an impish deed.

Everything was joyful and so special,
    Like the fun one gives a holiday,
And that which might become methodical,
    Was hidden in a rousing roundelay.

The pansies wore a smile upon their face,
    So happy to maintain their blooms so long,
But then, nothing here was commonplace,
    At eve they even hummed a vesper song.

Then suddenly there was a stilly hush,
    (You know the feeling when ply is at its peak.)
A maiden, with a gown to match her blush,
    Approached the children in a manner meek.

You could see their spirits take a leap,
    Who could miss the flash of eagerness?
Besides, children's thoughts are hard to keep,
    When their joyful spirits effervesce.

They waited eager for their story time,
    In a casual setting marked out plain
By the ringing of the bluebell's chime,
    And seven circling pines for their domain.

It was no wonder that a musing poet,
    Was lured to thoughts of love with such a scene,
And noticing one certain dancer, let
    His mind run to her in the evergreen.

156

But there was much to ponder in this garden,
　　With so many things to catch one's eye,
So his poet mind reached quickly for his pen,
　　To record the beauty and so versify,

While he waited patient for the lass
　　To complete the children's story hour,
And hoped in finishing that she would pass,
　　Where he sat writing verses in the bower,

But listened more for footsteps on the lawn,
　　Than to meters measured out in lines
Like stars that come, then vanish with the dawn,
　　When a greater spectrum overshines.

At last she came upon the path where
　　He sat secluded, feigning contemplation
On his art, with his mind elsewhere,
　　In a self-imposed oblivion.

Her nature sensitive and so refined,
　　Responded (a bit surprised) to his presense
Rising somewhat hesitant, behind
　　The peach rose with its tantalizing essence.

"I am so sorry, sir, to intrude
　　Upon your reverie," she calmly said,
"And upon this place of solitude
　　Which the rose and vine have garlanded."

He answered quickly lest she turn away,
　　And he miss the charm of her sweet grace,
And the scent of the violet nosegay,
　　The children gave her in their trysting place.

"I could not call this meeting an intrusion,"
    He answered softly but with dignity,
For her presence was a pure libation,
    Flowing over his soliloquy.

"The pleasure would be mine if you but stayed
    And retraced the beauty of this place,
In the comfort of this scented shade,
    Where this rose and vine does interlace."

"I thank you kindly for your invitation.
    Sir," she said, "you speak earnestly
With compelling tones of adjuration,
    Spoken with poetic artistry,

"I would be more than happy to assist
    You, as we imbibe the essence of this bower."
Here, by a rose descending they were kissed
    With petals falling in a gentle shower.

But the shower had a deeper meaning,
    And for a moment each thought and felt as one
And each found themselves now entering
    Elysian Fields that lay below the sun.

Part VI. Elysian Fields

There were no gates to hint one might not enter,
though perimeters were marked in light,
as early evening clouds might gather 'round
a spreading sun in its declining moments,
then trail off into a cosmic blur.

158

This phenomena struck him foremost,
and for an instant searched the reason for it.
No time was there between the search and answer,
which needed not a space for contemplation;
the concept floated past him like a gentle
zephyr, then left its whispering breath to trail on,
as effortless he held the memory.
Leaning to his consort's slanted gaze,
he read with ease the thought she opened to him,
that in Elysian Fields all thought was pure,
nullifying any need for gates.

With shyness she gave answer to his question.
"The only barring is the love itself
that will not violate another's will,
or force entrance into another's mind."
As all good teachers may entice their charges
to augment a concept, she drooped her head
and briefly paused to give him space, to let
a flow of cosmic energies inspire.
Effortless he knew, that here, the only
door was will, hence, no need for symbols.
She sweetly smiled assent to grace his thought,
as a mother might approve her child's
sudden knowing with a gentle smile.
Delicate the peace that overflowed them,
lifting mind and spirit to completeness.

On this reverie a touch of earth
intruded to remind them of a goal.
In such a glorious freedom each did know
how sad it was that flesh had been a chain.

As they strolled amid Elysian Fields
the two hearts moving as one spirit doubled
too their pleasure, and every bloom their senses
lit upon, glowed with twice the radiance.
The rose and moss rose, pinks and deep-hued mullen,
left their scent upon them as they passed,
and with a nod the flowers dropped a pearl
into their palms and clearly each did bear
their name. They spoke them softly to each other;
she plainly heard, "Rayleen," and he heard "Curtis,"
and a listening angel recorded them
upon the ever floating ethers. In this
realm it was a sacred ritual.

One flower group unique from all the rest,
were as babes to others, and were shown
great tenderness. These were resurrections
from earth's gifts with love and honor give,
and bore proudly names of their blest givers.
Rayleen and Curtis touched them gently as those
in spirit worlds are wont to do; and they
in turn curtsied back in childish sweetness.
Elated by the gesture, they dropped a grateful
tear, and then strolled on to view the forest.

Delights were all about them but they chose
to linger 'mong the trees where the glitter
of an emerald sheen played games with their
own images cast upon the ground.
Enthralled were they with this interplay
while an angel left them to their gazing,
until a stirring of her wings brought
attention to her presence. This seraph clad
in blue and very tiny, perched upon

a branch, and told them of the emerald forest.
Her measured words were hardly said above
the breeze's whisper, and blue sapphires in her
tiara blazed the name of, Amethyst.
"You marvel at the emerald chips that glisten
in the sun, (yet need no sun to glisten)
for each leaf glows with virtue of its own
and each does represent an healing unguent.
All transmuted pain is manifested
in these enduring leaves. Within the core
of each an embryo of prayer was planted
and perpetually they gather light,
'til healing and the leaf are then complete."
Here they saw the principles of growth
much like the realm of earth, where first appears
a lesser growth and lesser too the glow
and character. Amethyst continued,
"The things beheld in this great realm
are repeated in all galaxies."
They questioned how these things could be on earth.
She did not ponder her reply but answered
forthright: "When pure love is bonded to
humility."

The angel pointing then
continued, "These small trees are but beginnings
of a prayer, and those that you see yonder
(that are large but to your eyes seem bare)
are for the healing of the nations. We wait
eager for this hope to manifest."
With a close look, they saw the swelling buds.
Both bowed their heads in profoundest grief,
for the sufferings of humanity,
hoping for the end of ugly strife

in wars, and treaties that have no germ of peace,
or selfish ends that have not charity.

A shadow crossed their faces, for they saw
the need for careful choices to be made,
Together, they now vowed devotion, to
a higher cause than human selfish aims.
After a ponderous moment both arose
hearing symphonic music of the masters
playing exquisitely beyond the trees.

Unexpectedly a joyous pulse
thrilled them when they came upon a lamb
and lion cub, romping in the grasses.
With extended arms they gathered them
upon their bosoms as you would gather children
running to you in a joyous greeting.
Fearlessly they stroked a silky mane
and a head akin to fine-spun wool.
Time here could not be segmented into
compartments, or limited by happenings,
but all moved ever onward rhythmically.

They wondered why so unawares a hunger
seized them, but almost in the selfsame instant
knew it came from deep within their natures.
Beyond the grassy fields they spied a full-grown
orchard and sighed as one, to see the distance
that needed to be traversed. But in the sigh
the inspiration to accomplish dissolved
the grassy lea between. They laughed together
at the miracle, and eagerly
they tried the fruit, moving quickly from
one luscious taste to test another. The size

and beauty was more like a vision that one
dreams and yet remained so very keen.
There was no process of decay, to mar
the fruit, and when picked replaced itself
completely without a time of arduous growth,
They were reminded that here no death existed.

Each became cognizant of a fervent
prayer, offered at a humble altar,
where in haunting strains it floated round
them from a distant past, reminding each
that soon their sojourn here would end. Two souls
awed and humble rose to meet the challenge,
while being enveloped in a sea of music,
humming in eternal sweetness, that even
highest angels tried but could not do.
Was it because the angels sometimes wept?
Who knows? For angels never tell they weep.
This music hummed in unison with stars and planets,
while marching through the galaxies unnumbered.

Majestically they kept a perfect rhythm
as though a metronome was clicking out
the beat. No sadness here nor could there be,
lest heaven itself descend into a lower
state, and jar the stars out from their courses.
"Ah, sweet mystery of life and love,"
(the theme of countless universes) was no
elusive secret in this blessedness.
The rests that came within the natural course
were filled with the wondrous depth of sound;
Aum, Aum, I AM, I AM, I AM,
and the altar angels echoed onward:
Aum, holy, holy is His name.

Both Curtis and his escort in stillest awe
breathed in the essence and breathed out the perfume
that their perfect harmony engendered.

Here and there some children gaily danced,
with the freedom children love so well,
and with each measured step they sang a hymn
To assist the swell and resonance.
The sojourn ended with two souls conscious
of their eternal journey round the sun,
ever mindful that each encircling round
brought transformation and extended vision.

Conclusion

Their bodies glided freely in the rapture
of the moment, then perceptively
they felt a trill pass through them thoroughly.
There was one parting kiss and their hands
unloosed their clasp. The rending of their hearts
rippled up the blue where even stars
trembled at the parting. In sadness they
descended from Elysian shores.

Was it
possible that heaven knew such sadness?
Had these celestial beings forsaken them?
This mystery was hard to understand,
though he had heard how angels often wept
when returning to their Father's throne.

164

Once more the poet was alone and left
to battle with himself, yet did retain
a memory to cherish and to aid him in his
inspiration. He found himself returned
to the brookside where he had struggled,
but now the angel gone, gone too the altar,
gone the graceful dancer, gone his beloved.
Also gone the teachers and (should we say)
gone too the lessons learned. The whisperings of
a promise haunted him that one day all
would be fulfilled. He now picked up his latent pen
and feverishly began to write.